ROOTS HOME

Gillian Clarke, National Poet of Wales 2008–2016, President of Tŷ Newydd, the Welsh Writers Centre. Awarded the Queen's Gold Medal for Poetry in 2010. Her *Selected Poems* was published by Picador in 2016, and *Zoology*, her ninth collection from Carcanet, in 2017. Her version of the seventh-century Welsh poem *Y Gododdin* appears from Faber in 2021. She lives on a smallholding in Ceredigion, where in 2019, six acres were planted up with woodland.

also by Gillian Clarke, from Carcanet

Zoology
Ice
A Recipe for Winter
At the Source
Letter from a Far Country
Making the Beds for the Dead
Five Fields
Collected Poems
Selected Poems
The King of Britain's Daughter
Letting in the Rumour

Roots Home

Essays and a Journal

Gillian Clarke

CARCANET

First published in Great Britain in 2021 by
Carcanet
Alliance House, 30 Cross Street
Manchester M2 7AQ
www.carcanet.co.uk

A CIP catalogue record for this book is available from the British Library.

ISBN 978 1 80017 078 0

Book design by Andrew Latimer
Printed in Great Britain by SRP Ltd, Exeter, Devon

MIX
Paper from responsible sources
FSC® C014540

The publisher acknowledges financial assistance from Arts Council England.

Supported using public funding by
ARTS COUNCIL ENGLAND

CONTENTS

ROOTS HOME

WHY I WRITE

A pencil, a pen, a page. In town, at railway stations, airports, it is the stationers that draws me. The ranks of pens, pencil sets, reams of paper, a red notebook with a hard cover, a ribbon to mark the page, an elastic band to keep its contents safe. I must have it, just in case. I am travelling. What if I fill the one I am using? In those circumstances, on the road and homesick already, one more new notebook is irresistible. It is more than need. It is desire, for another unruled Moleskine for notes, research, for trying a line; desire for a new ruled, spiral-bound A5 for draft after draft of a poem; for yet another little black A6 art book with acid-free paper to write my journal in minuscule longhand at about thirty-five closely written lines a page – my current little black journal is number fifty. Before discovering these perfect art books, I used whatever notebook took my fancy, since I was given a five-year diary for Christmas when I was fifteen.

Morning begins with my journal. I write in it most days, though not every day. It is friend and listener, to record, remember, rage and rhapsodise, a place for requiem and celebration. Words hold detail which might be forgotten – the way the hare halted as it crossed the lawn, the field where a rainbow touched down across the valley, the different voices of wind, or water, the close and distant territorial arias of May blackbirds. One night many years ago, when our house was still a ruin, used only for summer camping, as we stepped out into the pitch-dark garden we saw green lights, like searchlights, wavering in the north-eastern sky. The midnight news confirmed it was the aurora borealis, recorded in my little black book with all the rest, trivia, weather and wonders. I write to remember, to record the smallest thing.

But before meaning, before writing, a word is a sound. It is voiced, sung, spoken, single and slow, by someone leaning over a cot or a pram, smiling and mouthing a word, or a little rush of words, a phrase, a sentence; or the mysterious music of nursery rhymes. We love the sound of words before we understand them. I loved them *because* I could not understand them. I liked the pattern they made in books *before* I could write them. I mimicked words I heard. Family legend tells that I was heard chanting and stamping out the rhythm to these words: 'Ga puts Mentholatum on her sciatica, and Ceri soaks the clothes in Parazone.' Ga was my grandmother, Ceri my aunt. I collected strange words grown-ups used. I scribbled pretend 'words' on my bedroom wall through the bars of my cot. The wall was an empty page. Even now, setting down the first, uncertain words when beginning a poem, I feel the seduction of a new page. Describing his writing process, the poet R.S. Thomas said that he took a pen and paper to see what words would do. The child, scribbling on a bedroom wall or a page, is doing what a poet does. The child's first scribbled attempt at a word is primitive and instinctive. It is early man's mark on a cave wall. You can see what R.S. Thomas meant by 'seeing what words will do'.

I recently read of research into the development of language in babies. Scientists tested the babies' brain-reaction to the sound of a word and to the object it named. The babies connected the word with the object, listened and watched the speaker, responding to the spoken word. Some time passed before each baby's first attempt to say the word. It was concluded that a baby thinks about the word long before trying to say it.

I love that! Of course it does. The unspoken word is like the not yet articulated poem that awaits the pen, or the thought unspooling into a sentence in an essay or an article ready for the pen or tapped keys to let it grow, to stir, to become a human communication. It is like the brilliant line you think before you sleep, sure that you will remember it long enough to write it down in the morning. But by morning it has melted away, like the dream you forget the minute you are really awake. You need the pen, the scrap of paper, to keep it. I remember the poet, Irina Ratushinskaya, explaining how, in her Soviet prison cell, she wrote her poems by scratching them in soap before memorising them. Once written, typed, scratched in soap, crayoned on a wall, once they have a shape and a sound, they are real. You'll remember them then, more or less, if the page blows away in the wind.

Sylvia Plath, in 'Morning Song', describes her baby trying her first 'handful of notes', as 'clear vowels' rising 'like balloons.' A baby's first consonant is often 'm'. Is that the source of Mam, Mum, Mama, that almost universal word? My husband's aunt, Gwyneth Myfanwy, living contentedly in a care home in her nineties, suddenly stopped talking, or responding to talk. She slept a lot, and seemed preoccupied by vivid dreams. She was often heard calling out: 'Mam! Oh Mam', as if reliving her life and her childhood in her mind, calling, recalling, the mother she had cared for until *her* death aged a hundred and two. A few days later, Gwyneth died.

Might her last word, Mam, also have been her first? When we die, will losing the *world* precede losing the first and last *word*, as it seemed to do for Gwyneth Myfanwy, drowsing into a dream where all our words migrate from the borders of consciousness as life fades into silence?

After the word, the song and the rhyme, come stories, told and read aloud: my father's retelling of traditional Welsh legends from the *Mabinogi* when we were on a ramble or on the road in the car, the bedtime stories my mother told me, pointing to each word as she read. I heard the sound, and saw the shape her finger showed me. A child soon tries the sound that belongs to the known shape. Familiar words are repeated, favourite stories told and retold. That early pleasure in repeated sounds, in short, echoing word groups, in spells, in rhymes, in legends where choices come in sets of three, as well as the mysterious music of nursery rhymes, are the makings of the literate person. In my case they were surely leading to the art of writing, and the love of and practice of poetry.

I don't remember being *taught* to read. My mother read me stories, and as she read her finger followed the words, so I could hear the sound of each word-shape. Sentences and paragraphs guide the reader's path through prose. A poem's music is shaped by lines and verses. The form informs, tells us how to hear. The poem's shape on the page is the sound you hear. A poem is like a page of music. The line is the bar line. It carries the word-music of poetry.

Before I was born, my father had travelled the world with the merchant navy, a wireless officer with the Marconi company, until his radio skills and bilingualism brought him a job as a broadcasting engineer at the BBC in Wales. In his radio cabin on board ship, tapping spells in Morse code, he sent messages across oceans: storm warnings, sightings of icebergs or wreckage. The radio transmitted cries for help, ships in distress heard too far off course to assist, as messages passed ship to ship, ocean to ocean across the world between men like him, nicknamed as 'Sparks', in their subterranean cabins. As I write, I remember how exciting it was to be told how, decades before the internet, the international language of Morse could cross the world, travel all round the globe which I loved to spin in the corner of my bedroom. Morse code was another magic alphabet which, much later, my father tried to teach me.

I remember 'writing', or scribbling, with a pencil my father had sharpened to a dangerously perfect point. My parents must have forgiven my graffiti and trusted my tool management because soon after the pencil, I was given a pen, and guided to drawing and writing paper. Above the hinged lid of my child-size desk was a shallow depression to lay the pen down between dips into the tiny inkwell. One Christmas I had a real fountain pen, a Conway Stewart in marbled green with a gold nib like a blackbird's beak, nested in its own box; a bottle of blue Quink; proper notepaper with envelopes to match. I was seven. My mother thought it high time I wrote proper thank you letters.

Since then, no day is ever quite right without opening my journal to record, in black ink on a white page, the ordinary and the extraordinary, the weather, the world's mood, the April return of the swallows, their flights over the garden, the mud-cup of a nest in our porch, a gather of goldfinches, a flaunt of red kites over the field. I write because the page is a friend.

April has turned to May. This is a memory: walking the fields to feed the twin lambs of a ewe who had not quite enough milk for her growing twins. The lambs ran towards me while she watched, wary, but without fear. They nuzzled my pockets for their bottles, and soon emptied one each. The ewe called, and they returned to her. She nuzzled them to suckle her too, keeping the bond strong between them. We kept an eye on them, brought a bucket of sheep nuts for the ewe, a bottle for the lambs. But we are mere humans. The chemistry of the flock is mysterious and animal, and we are not part of it. I recall feeling a surge of joy at her trust and theirs, at that deep, inherited knowledge of where they belonged and what belonged to them: in Welsh it is known as *cynefin*. Joy too, which I share with my journal, at the greening of the avenue of twenty-four hornbeams we had planted in the last week of the last year of the last millennium. They were leafless sticks. Soon they scrawled leafy shadows on the grass between the two rows. Now they touch overhead, a green arcade. If I write it, here, in my journal, it is twice enjoyed. Because I write, I remember. Writing of events close to their happening involves a wide-awake mind and all senses alert in an effort to tell it true. To reread the journal is to live it again, more profoundly, given time to think. Poetry is a rhythmic way of thinking. If, in this reflective moment, a poem starts into life, a note in a journal opens itself to be shared with a reader. The hare in the gap, for example: the sudden heat of it, its breath, quiver, stillness, its *aliveness* saying, 'you too are alive'. It records the nowness of now, the moment completely lived.

I felt every bit of me awake as I watched the hare, but a poem wasn't ready. Literature was ready though. I recalled a brilliant few pages in one of Dylan Thomas's stories, 'The Peaches', with a marvellous description of a child's experience of consciousness. He writes of how alive he had felt, a boy playing wild games with a friend at his Aunt Annie's farm, Fern Hill (which he calls 'Gorsehill' in the story) and how, and I quote: 'I felt all my young body like an excited animal surrounding me, the torn knees bent, the bumping heart', and 'I was aware of me myself in the exact middle of a living story, and my body was my adventure and my name'.

'In the exact middle of a living story'! 'My body was my adventure and my name'! How I identify with that rich description of consciousness, of the aware young writer listening for language, alert for the truth of things.

Is consciousness a special human thing? My hare looked just as alive, as aware as I. Growing older, losing friends, the deaths of poets, sharpens consciousness and my need to write, to remember everything. In a poem written after the far too early death of my friend, the poet Frances Horovitz, I say: 'I must write like the wind, year after year / passing my death-day, winning ground'. I often find myself saying, these days, after the deaths of Seamus Heaney, Dennis O'Driscoll, Dannie Abse, and others, 'I must write like the wind', 'winning ground'.

The act of writing involves not just observed experience, but reflection, remembering and recording. Nothing must pass unseen, unheard. The pen itself plumbs a poet's energy. It is a rod to touch the wire between brain and word. The electric flash it makes is the first spark of a poem. Maybe the act of writing the journal sends a message home to the heart and out to the stars – like my father's Morse code crossing oceans – field to house, journal to Moleskine, and on to the thrill of a poem's first line, its first draft. The touch of pen on paper. But here is a contradiction. I write this on a laptop computer. I look up and see miles of hill country – as I do every morning – look down, and write. A poem is physical. I often first half-dream a poem and fall asleep hoping I'll remember it. Then, only the pen can remember. Today, walking back from the fields, the dreamed ideas returned. Had a poem been brewing, I could not have begun without a pen. But this is not the hot spark of a poem, this is prose, the fast-flowing water of the mind. This goes smoother, quicker, more like speech, like breathing, or walking, less like the poem's first wordless sounding of the deep, or a stone thrown into space. The poem, like drawing, needs the pen to see what words will do. It begins as an abstract thing, a body-and-mind sensation, like a not-quite-grasped concept in physics, mathematics, or faith. It is literally 'at the back of the mind', as if, could you turn quickly enough, you would catch it. Prose is like speech, and the speed of its flow goes faster on the computer. I write this to order thought. To write poem or prose I need weather and sky. I look up, observe, think. Prose runs as fast as thought. Prose is the hare racing the wind. The poem is the hare that halts on the lawn.

'TRAMP. NOTHING IS UNTIL IT HAS A WORD'

I want to begin with the word 'nothing', but *something* won't go away. I am eleven years old. I pedal up Plymouth Road, Penarth, on a summer Saturday morning. My daps are a dazzle of Blanco dried in the sun on the kitchen step. Mown grass, the powdery smell of blancoed daps, warm tar of the road. The spin of bicycle wheels. It feels like freedom.

I pick up shopping for my mother from the grocer, drop my bike outside the library, shoulder a bag of books and step into the shadow of the porch. The library is my Aladdin's cave, my Secret Garden, my Treasure Island. I'm bringing six books back, and I'll take six away. I feel excited. There's a book I specially want and I can't wait to get my hands on it. The library is a world of books, and every book is a world. Although it's a public library, it's my private place.

We had books at home: children's books that were birthday or Christmas presents, A.A. Milne, Walter de la Mare, Arthur Ransome, Lewis Carroll; the William books, and Enid Blyton; *Palgrave's Golden Treasury*; Grimm's *Fairy Tales*; Arthur Mee's *Children's Encyclopaedia*; a brown and gold set of hardback Charles Dickens, the Brontës, and books my father loved like *Moby Dick*, Jack London's *Call of the Wild* and *White Fang*. I read them all, over and over. Mostly, we used the library. No house could ever have satisfied my desire for books, or provided me with the frisson of finding for myself slightly risqué romances, like Ethel M. Dell, and E.M. Hull's *The Sheik*, hiding on the shady shelves of the library, and books whose titles and authors I forget, but whose pages, people and atmospheres I still inhabit, as they inhabit me. Sometimes,

I feel I'm stepping suddenly into a remembered room, with an open piano, maybe, a chair, a view, a familiar ambiance, or rowing over water to an island, or walking a path to the sea. Someone is with me, ahead or following. Who? Did I *live* that memory? Is it real? Or did I read it in a book?

In the first two minutes I've used three words that are on their way to nothing. Daps. Blanco. Grocer. Dying words. A word needs a meaning to pass between speaker and listener, writer and reader, or it'll come to nothing. Sheenagh Pugh's 'Elegy for the Dead Words' is written in the voice of an old teacher forced to emigrate, one future day, along with all Earth's inhabitants, to a neighbouring planet. The poem laments the loss of words for all the things left behind. After a lovely litany of favourite words, the poem concludes: 'Things that are dead we keep with words, but when the words die themselves; oh then they're dead, and dead indeed'.

Dead words still have a ring about them when they leave common speech. They hold history, words no longer used or needed, words whose objects and purpose are gone, flicker and die, unheard, unread. 'Daps' (as we say in Wales) have become 'trainers', and I think the 'Blanco' with which we whitened them, before putting them on the step to dry in the sun, has gone too. Such words slip painlessly into silence, leaving our tongues long before they leave our memory, to be lost in word-history.

While tutoring poetry I often illustrate my sermon against latinates with this example: 'I was proceeding along the highway when I perceived two persons', seventeen syllables which I imagine spoken by a policeman bearing witness in court to impress the judge and jury. Translated into words a poet might speak cuts it to ten syllables: 'I walked down the road and I saw two men'.

Gone the pompous 'proceeded', 'highway', 'perceived', 'persons', replaced by 'walked', 'road', 'saw', 'men'. Even children guess the fictional speaker correctly, they know the difference between plain truth and elaboration. Compare the poetry of the authorised King James translation of the Bible with the prosaic literalism of the New English version.

Now words face a new danger: the Word Police, busy 'correcting' the language in an effort to control our thoughts and attitudes. They mean well, they don't set out to lie or to silence poetry, but it is happening. As a poet I know that when our simple Anglo-Saxon words, whose sound and meaning speak plainly, are replaced by multisyllabic latinates, the intention and effect are to hide, to forget. The phrase 'collateral damage', denying the murder of innocent civilians in the Second World War, and again during the Gulf War of 1991, is an example. When those in control speak words no one trusts, truth dies, replaced by the rattle of latinate lies.

For those obsessed with 'political correctness' the blind and the deaf become 'visually' or 'aurally impaired'. I wear hearing aids, my magic microphones. I am a bit deaf, not aurally impaired. Rightly banished are inaccurate, insulting words describing people with physical or mental conditions, words like 'cripple' and 'lunatic', scientifically incorrect, born of bigotry. Good riddance to them.

But this morning, doing the *Guardian* crossword set by 'Tramp' has me musing on good lost words, those we still need to tell our story, now endangered by the Word Police. I consider these things because I have suffered my first-ever act of censorship, and it is painful. My hurt is caused by the cutting of a word. The sentence where my word appears, and the man it describes, is heard in my voice-over for a short film, one of a series called 'Revealing Wales' made for the Royal Society of Architects in Wales.

I first wrote my piece as an essay commissioned by the RSAW, and it was published without fuss in 2016 as my preface to the book on Cardiff Civic Centre by John Hilling.

It was well received by the author, the RSAW, and the publisher, the University of Wales Press. The film-makers invited me to record the essay as a voice-over for their film on Cardiff Civic Centre, a harmonious arrangement of fine white buildings along two wide, tree-lined avenues among parkland, a place I have known and loved all my life, especially as an undergraduate at the University.

I recorded the piece. The film was made. It is beautiful. Then down the line from someone titled Head of Content – a perfect example of pompous latinate language – at the Royal Institute of British Architects' head office in London came the diktat: delete one word or we ban the film. My word was blue-pencilled – RIBA head office wields financial power over the RSAW.

I am careful with my words. They are my tools, my art, my truth, the stuff of the profession in which I am trusted: I see the cut as a dangerous intrusion into free speech, freedom of thought, word choice, and the long story of literature in which I play my small part. The offending word, the good, true word, for which there is no substitute, is in the opening paragraph, in which I list people I remember, people with whom I spoke, with whom I had shared the beauty of trees and lawns and white stone buildings. One was: 'The tramp asleep on a bench in the park'.

'Tramp' offended the Head of Content at the RIBA. My tramp is a real, remembered person, the only individual mentioned in the list of those I recall in the Civic Centre's parks and gardens. He is there for his own sake. Reading English in the University, I passed him as I walked through the park to lectures. 'Morning,' we'd say, with a nod and a smile. I once shared my sandwiches with him. Another time he said: 'Been tramping west for the turnips. Nice to be back in Cardiff.'

He was a man with 'time to stand and stare',[1] and his example taught me to do so too. Tramping was his chosen way of life. He was not a walker, a traveller, a vagrant, a rough sleeper, nor any other inaccurate term or euphemism. He was a tramp, but my use of this simple, honest, single-syllable word was banned by the London office of the RIBA. Unless the word were cut from my voice-over, London would withdraw the money, and Wales and the RSAW would lose the film. It is an illiterate, urban judgment. Yet I think of great architecture as a kind of truth, as 'poetry in stone', just as poetry is truth in word-music. Both arts should despise passing fashion and 'political correctness', and speak plain truth.

Tramp. No word comes to mind without bringing its ambiance, association, story. My word has no fitting synonym. It is a word still understood by all those to whom I tell this sorry story. It belongs to a time and a place when men such as my tramp travelled the roads, to be welcomed as seasonal workers on farms, to be offered a meal and space to sleep in a barn or a hayloft, as welcome as the troubadours with their songs in medieval times. Tramp, the verb, and tramp, the noun, name a way of life and the man who lived it.

In 2017 I took part in a festival of Celtic music and poetry in Glasgow, organised by Celtic Connections. The festival theme was 'Stand and Stare', quoted from W.H. Davies's poem, 'Leisure', set as a beautiful song, and movingly performed:

> What is this life if, full of care,
> We have no time to stand and stare? –
>
> No time to stand beneath the boughs,
> And stare as long as sheep and cows:

---

1 'Leisure' by W.H. Davies.

No time to see, when woods we pass,
Where squirrels hide their nuts in grass:

No time to see, in broad daylight,
Streams full of stars, like skies at night:

No time to turn at Beauty's glance,
And watch her feet, how they can dance:

No time to wait till her mouth can
Enrich that smile her eyes began?

A poor life this if, full of care,
We have no time to stand and stare.

W.H. Davies identified himself as a tramp. I have an ancestor who sometimes tramped with the poet. My husband's great-uncle tramped between Ceredigion and South Wales for work. Here in Ceredigion, I used to see a tramp on a bicycle, all his earthly goods hanging from its frame, who sheltered close by in an empty thatch-roofed cottage when passing through. He was a *crwydryn*, a tramp; if he stayed in one place too long he got itchy feet. He loved to *crwydro* Wales, working where he could. Such men were valuable seasonal labourers.

One day, when I was young and lived at home in Penarth, a few miles from Cardiff, I waved to a man walking out of our drive into the lane called Tower Hill. He had been doing some gardening for us. Later that evening my mother sent me to fetch apples from the loft over the garage. There, beside the rows of fruit laid down to store for winter, I found a dinner plate licked clean on the floor beside an old mattress. I told my father. 'Sh!' he said. 'Don't tell your mother!' A tramp had eaten and slept well that night, and I was happy.

Here, in Ceredigion, as well as in the city where I used to live, 'tramp' is a good word, used and understood along with its Welsh form, *crwydryn, crwydro*. A friend, a farmer's daughter, hearing my complaint, responded with warmth: 'Oh yes,' she said, 'I remember tramps coming regularly to the farm to ask for work. My father was glad of them, and they got a meal and a night's shelter and some cash.'

To kill a word is to kill truth, as writers have always known. To censor the tramp and his story is to pretend that he never existed. But he'll be back. He will not be cleansed from history, from his place in the sun, napping on a bench in the park, or pausing to stand and stare. W.H. Davies identified himself as a tramp. What's next for the word-killers? Will they burn all copies of his *Autobiography of a Super-Tramp*?

Children love words, the sound and taste, the tune and the mystery. They love tonguing the word, trying it out loud in mispronunciation, in rhyme, nonsense and naughtiness, those words they hear the grown-ups use. Early readers mispronounce the words they meet for the first time on a page: '*izland*' and '*Percy-phone* in the Underworld' were among my mistakes. Even in my A-level English class I was caught out by 'mis-led'. '*Mizled*', I read aloud, with a long 'i'. They laughed at me, but added to the humiliation was my grief for the verb '*to mizle*', which held more deceit, more spin than 'misled'. It half-rhymes with *weasel*. I grieve for it still. I feel '*mizled*' by the weasel words of our politicians rather than simply 'mis-led'.

Nursery rhymes are the first poetry. They have everything necessary to qualify as great poems. They stay in the memory. They have rhythm and rhyme, mystery, strangeness, and a thrilling vocabulary a four-year-old doesn't understand. Words like *janitor*, and *sentinel*. As in, 'I'm in love with the janitor's boy and he's in love with me', or 'There was an old woman who lived in a wood – and an owl at the door as sentinel stood'.

Later, when I became a mother, my elderly Auntie Phyllis came to stay. My three young children ran about the house giggling and chanting 'Phyllis is a billis'. She expressed delight at their joy in the rhyming game – and I agreed with her. I did not explain that 'billis' was the children's word for a penis. Such assonance and alliteration were the Beano and Dandy school of poetry, fun, pun and rhyme. Pansy Potter the Strong Man's Daughter and the whole comic crew of alliteratively named characters. It was a good chapter in my and my children's education, a poet's apprenticeship, the years between nursery rhymes and Shakespeare. It sang alongside playground games, chanting, nicknames, dipping and spells. If it works, poetry is always a kind of spell. It was the same Aunt, railway clerk from Carmarthen, with little formal education behind her, who fell in love with words herself in her girlhood, reading her way along the public-library shelves, eventually to be stunned by the miracle of Shakespeare. It was she who took me, aged ten, to the old Memorial Theatre in Stratford to see *King Lear*, and to every subsequent production until I was twenty-two. Because she was 'hard of hearing', we sat in the first row of the stalls, close enough to see the sparkle of the actors' spit in the spotlights. Theatre was bigger, brighter, louder than life. Yet it was a world I knew – of battles of will between father and daughter, of sulks and sisters and family rows – but more so. Books, then, seemed more real than life.

There, in the theatre, where the characters were live people, my whole body listened. I was eavesdropping on the grown-ups, as I did all the time at home. I'd learned to read their white lies, their whispers, their 'not in front of the child!' Here, on stage, was an old father showing up his daughter in front of everyone; and a girl too embarrassed, too angry, too sulky to say something just to please him. I knew the scene. The music of the language shaped the game they played with words like 'nothing'. I had it by heart from that hour:

Lear: Now, our joy.
Although our last and least, to whose young love
The vines of France and milk of Burgundy
Strive to be interess'd, what can you say to draw
A third more opulent than your sisters'? Speak.
Cordelia: Nothing, my Lord.
Lear: Nothing!
Cordelia: Nothing.
Lear: Nothing will come of nothing, speak again.

My ten-year-old self in the front row felt sorry for both of them, the 'foolish, fond old man', the stubborn daughter. I *was* Cordelia. He was my father. Their words, their voices, have stayed in my mind ever since. Years later, when Sam Wanamaker, editing an anthology to help raise funds to rebuild Shakespeare's Globe Theatre, commissioned me to write a poem, remembering every detail, every word of that night, I wrote 'Llŷr', giving Lear the name of the Welsh king who inspired Shakespeare's character:

'and there I heard
That nothing is until it has a word.'

With a bit of luck, the right words come from the very stuff of the language around us, in our heads, our ears, enriched by listening and reading, nourished by the voices of poets living and dead. Words, especially the words that drop into your mind or off your pen onto the page as if appearing out of nowhere, are the gift a shared language brings. The English language we speak is full of quotations, whether or not we know it, and the dead poets contributed most of them. No poem written now lacks the echo of all the poems ever heard or read, reverberating in our collective mind. No poem is the only poem. Poetry should come naturally to everyone, the fun of word-song, the pleasure of listening and reading, the consolation and humanity of it. Poetry sings in the cadences of common speech, overheard and picked up, a coin found on the pavement. My best eavesdropping moment gave me a little poem called 'Overheard in County Sligo'. I stole the first two lines, spoken at the Yeats School in Sligo by a local Irish woman to an American academic. She explained how she lost her chance to audition for the Abbey Theatre in Dublin. Her words were poetry:

I married a man from County Roscommon
And I live in the back of beyond

Truth, in ordinary human language, is poetry. A woman interviewed on radio after an earthquake in South America described the experience: 'The earth shook its skin like an old horse.' A bereaved mother declared, after her son died in a sectarian murder in Ireland: 'Let no mother's son be killed for my boy. Let's have an end to all the mourning and the weeping.'

We name to articulate the world and its infinite detail. First, as babies, we learn to name things. Then come questions, doubt, lies, wonder, anticipation. Once, in Snowdonia, as we stopped to park by a lake, my twenty-month-old daughter woke suddenly in the car. She gasped at what she saw through the car window, and uttered what was probably her very first sentence: 'Look – at all the mountains I think.' The key word is '*think*'. Nothing is until it has a word. She found words to wonder, to suppose, to name what she had only seen in picture books. She knew the difference. The conscious *person* was waking in a baby, through language.

Poets are the language-makers: from Anon to Shakespeare, the small and the great, poets of the people, poets of the canon, of the library since the sixth century when Taliesin and

Aneirin made their verse in the dawning poetic tradition in these islands of Britain, when Welsh *was* the British language, and English not yet formed.

It's lucky for us that the poets of medieval England chose the many-stranded dialect of ordinary English to make their poems. It's thanks to the balladeers, troubadours, itinerant wordsmiths and, finest of all, Chaucer, that English survived. He could have chosen Norman French, the language of power, court and class. So the Middle English of his day thrived and grew into the rich language we speak now, the lingua franca of millions, with the biggest dictionary of all, packed with words stolen from French, Welsh, Latin and many other tongues, and it still steals more words every year. A generation earlier, the great Welsh poet, Dafydd ap Gwilym, travelling Europe as a 'troubadour', brought home a wealth of new vocabulary and ideas which, through his poetry, were soon absorbed into Welsh. Through literature language is preserved and refreshed. Welsh, safekeeper of one of Europe's oldest literatures, is alive and flourishing. In Welsh, nothing at all is *dim byd* – literally, 'no world'.

Poetry has other less grown-up purposes: it's for getting a child up the wooden hill to bed; it's for cutting a baby's finger- and toenails with a rhyme – 'one little piggy went to market'; it's 'dipping' to decide who goes first, who's in, who's out; it keeps the beat in skipping and circle-games; it's for remembering how to spell 'difficulty', (D, I, FFI, C,U, LTY) or 'beautiful', or 'i before e except after c'; it's for counting miles between the flash of lightning and the growl of thunder. It's for falling asleep. It's for learning by heart so that you own a work of art which you can take with you anywhere as long as you live. The last thing on your mind before you die could be a line of verse.

The GCSE English exam and the internet bring teenagers all over the world to poetry. This audience comes to my screen at the press of a button, without subsidy, cost or hassle. As exam day approaches, the trickle of teenage requests for help with a poem grows to a swarm. They deserve answers, and I feel honoured that a few of my poems are briefly a part of their lives. I see it as a teaching job, payback for the good teaching I had. I direct students with the simplest questions to prepared notes on my website, but sometimes a poetry lesson is needed. One poem, set for the Oxford and Cambridge international English exam, brings questions from all over the world, in just two weeks from Kuwait, Dubai, Mumbai, Pakistan, Ghana, Mexico, New Zealand, Canada, China, Bahrain, Singapore. The poem is 'Lament'. Its subject, the first Gulf War.

One day I received an email from Emmanuel Owoniyi, of Accra, Ghana, in teenage textspeak: 'lament got me raise my hand in lit. class and actually say someth that made sense in d class.... Thx 4 lament'.

I replied that he should raise his hand in lit class every time he had an idea. A few days later I had another message from Emmanuel. I copy it here exactly:

> I got homework please.?? Quote: 'read the poem 'lament', comment on the tone. Is it sad or angry, does it change as it progresses. Show how the poet *thats you :) :D* communicates to you'. i am nt that good in lit. I will really appreciate it if you help me here.

I sent Emmanuel a little poetry lesson. I hoped he got a good grade. The poem that bemused him was written in response to news of the first Gulf War, 1990 to 1991. Iraq invaded Kuwait, the US sent troops. Britain joined in. Recently, I heard from a man who served in the Royal Navy at the time, part of Britain's involvement in the war. He said he had suffered from post-traumatic stress ever since, unable to talk about it until his daughter studied 'Lament' for her GCSE exams. Her

English syllabus used my poem, written in response to news of the war. At last, he could talk about what the war had done to him. They read the poem together, he shared his memories, flashbacks, nightmares. He wrote to me, grateful that a poem had given him a way to talk to her of his experience, at last hopeful of finding healing.

Lament

For the green turtle with her pulsing burden
in search of the breeding ground.
For her eggs laid in their nest of sickness.

For the cormorant in his funeral silk,
the veil of iridescence on the sand,
the shadow on the sea.

For the ocean's lap with its mortal stain.
For Ahmed at the closed border.
For the soldier in his uniform of fire.

For the gunsmith and the armourer,
the boy fusilier who joined for the company,
the farmer's sons, in it for the music.

For the hook-beaked turtles,
the dugong and the dolphin,
the whale struck dumb by the missile's thunder.

For the tern, the gull and the restless wader,
the long migrations and the slow dying,
the veiled sun and the stink of anger.

For the burnt earth and the sun put out
The scalded ocean and the blazing well.
For vengeance, and the ashes of language.

A few years ago I heard from Yasmeen Khan, a teacher from Mianwali, Pakistan. She asked me for help with a poem her class was studying. 'The Field Mouse', written in the 1990s at the time of the war in Bosnia, was commissioned by the editor of an anthology against war. The poem is set in Ceredigion, haymaking on a summer day at the same time as war raged in Bosnia, where over 8,000 Muslim men and boys were murdered in Srebrenica. Ratko Mladić, responsible for that genocide, free for many years, was caught at last and tried in The Hague. The poem was studied by GCSE students for years, but for me it seemed, suddenly, to have new meaning. Yasmeen's last message concluded: 'I could teach them peace through your poem. Thanks and love from all of us. Yasmeen.' Peace, one to one across nation, class, race, religion, and all that would divide us. There is no better reason to write or read a poem.

The Field Mouse

Summer, and the long grass is a snare drum.
The air hums with jets.
Down at the end of the meadow,
far from the radio's terrible news,
we cut the hay. All afternoon
its wave breaks before the tractor blade.
Over the hedge our neighbour travels his field
in a cloud of lime, drifting our land
with a chance gift of sweetness.

The child comes running through the killed flowers,
his hands a nest of quivering mouse,
its black eyes two sparks burning.
We know it'll die and ought to finish it off.
It curls in agony big as itself
and the star goes out in its eye.
Summer in Europe, the fields hurt,
and the children kneel in long grass
staring at what we have crushed.

Before day's done the field lies bleeding,
the dusk garden inhabited by the saved, voles,
frogs, a nest of mice. The wrong that woke
from a rumour of pain won't heal,
and we can't face the newspapers.
All night I dream the children dance in grass
their bones brittle as mouse ribs, the air
stammering with gunfire, my neighbour turned
stranger, wounding my land with stones.

SLATE

It is almost Christmas, I am three years old, and we have come to stay at my maternal grandparents' farm in north-east Wales, between the River Dee and the Berwyn hills. Top Farm, Rhosddu, Wrexham. In the big farm kitchen, my Taid[1] smokes his pipe in the wing chair on the right-hand side of the range. In the scullery across the passage my Nain[2] is plucking the goose. She stands in a snowstorm of feathers falling around her onto the huge slate slabs of the floor. My mother's youngest sister, Elen, sweeps them into a drift in the corner to gather and save for pillows and feather beds. Then she fills a tin pail at the sink, and flings a wave of soapy water over the slate floor. It darkens to purple. The suds are swept out of the door, down the passage, into the yard, and the floor dries slowly to lavender.

Slate is our stone, from the quarries of Snowdonia. The coal in the grate is ours too, from the South Wales Coalfield. We tread on slate every day. Penrhyn slate, from Bethesda, Snowdon, Eryri, mount of eagles. It floors Top Farm's *beudy*[3] too, where the cows sway home, clattering and slipping on the slates morning and evening, each to her own stall, for milking. Next to the scullery is the dairy. The dairy slab is a huge unbroken slice of mountain. Like the dairy and larder slabs in all the neighbouring farms, it is ice-cold, and it keeps cool the churns, jugs and bowls of milk, their cream rising. There's a fat pat of butter too, fresh from churning and printed

---

1 north Welsh for grandfather.

2 north Welsh for grandmother.

3 cowshed.

with a sheaf of wheat, and the cold corpse of the goose-fleshy goose, plucked, stuffed and trussed for the oven.

In 1819, my young paternal great-great-grandfather, grandfather to my Tadcu,[1] was working the stone boats, loading slate from Caernarfon dock for the crossing to Anglesey. By the end of the nineteenth century Penrhyn, one of many slate quarries in Snowdonia, was the world's largest, worked by nearly 3,000 quarrymen. Slate sills, thresholds, floors, larder slabs, gravestones. Slabs wired as uprights for fences; two vertical and one horizontal for a stile; massive orthostats for gateposts; odd shapes set flat for a path from door to washing line. A tilted slab of slate under brambles and leaning trees in a derelict chapel graveyard is engraved with the names of my maternal great-grandparents. Then another stone, a clean slate slab upright in sunlight in mown grass, remembers my Nain[2] and Taid, he coming in from the yard, stamping mud off his boots on the threshold like a horse, she in the scullery, plucking, plucking.

In city, town, village and upland farm, we sleep under Welsh slate. Rain sings on it. It roofed every house I have ever lived in, and is over my head as I write these words. It helped power the Industrial Revolution. It roofs the terraced houses of much of Britain, draws the contour lines of valleys, delineating the curved streets of pit-villages climbing the mountain slopes.

Despite our twice-yearly family visits from Cardiff to visit Nain on the farm in Denbighshire – Taid died when I was three – I had never experienced the north-western mountains of Snowdonia until my father, a first-language Welsh-speaker from Carmarthenshire and a passionate Welshman, decided I should know the beauty and infinite variety of my country's landscape as well as its culture and its industrial

---

1 south Welsh for grandfather.

2 grandmother, North Wales.

history. When I was twelve he took me on a long drive north through Snowdonia. It was on that journey that I first saw the spectacular slate tips and quarries of Blaenau Ffestiniog and Bethesda, and some of the great waterfalls of the north. It was like first experiencing cubism after studying nineteenth-century landscape painting. The familiar earth had been taken apart, and its components, stone, water, weather, light, had been re-formed by a giant creator. It was, indeed, a terrible beauty. To this day the sight of slate-tips in rain never fails to fill me with awe, such an unbearable weight of angles and shards, of greys, purples, silvers, broken pieces of sky, so many deaths, so much lost life. So much geological and human history.

Eryri, mount of eagles, is Snowdon's true name. The eagles have gone, but we walk the mountain under the floating shadows of peregrine, chough, ring ouzel, hen harrier, merlin. The first time I climbed Snowdon it was a rare, fine day, the sun on our backs as we leaned to the slope, foot after foot, heaving our way to the summit, concentrating on the track beneath our feet, shale worn grassless by boot and hoof. Sometimes, needing to draw breath, needing to look, we paused, stood still and turned to the view. Was it that time – I can't be sure – that beyond unfolding peak after peak, there, stretched out before me, lay England, or at least the Cheshire Plain, reaching eastwards in a golden haze, with Wales all around me, and to the west the misty blues of the Irish Sea. Once, roughly following the train track down, I witnessed what is called a 'glory', an unbroken circular rainbow below in the mist of the Llanberis Pass. There the path runs vertiginously close to the edge, and below is nothing but the sheer drop of the mountain. Another time, after climbing for hours in rain, I saw skies clear to reveal a world simple as a map, from the misty distances of England to the mirage of Ireland, and Anglesey – Môn, mother of Wales – as if in a school atlas.

Alongside the track, in the grass, on slopes and in crevices, is beauty in miniature. Sometimes I have known the name of a tiny flower growing there, often not, though there are botanical treasures, mountain flowers growing in Arctic scree, in grains and dusts of sand, granite, quartzite, on precipice, crevice and grassy ledge, on the vertical rock walls of rivers and waterfalls: parsley fern, fir clubmoss, woolly fringe moss, liverwort, wavy hair grass, sheep's fescue, foxglove, heath bedstraw, heather, bilberry, myrtle, and crevice communities of ferns, mosses, lichens, arctic saxifrage, maidenhair, spleenwort, and the brittle blade fern.

Most special of all, unique to this place, in rocky clefts too steep for nibbling sheep, grows the Snowdon lily, a delicate white flower shivering in the wind. It has survived since the Ice Age on Snowdon's north-facing cliffs, the only Arctic-type rock-crevice conditions north of the Alps. It has evolved alone, a unique survivor. I have never seen it. I am content to imagine it, to believe in it, to relish its picture in the botanical guide, to enjoy its name, to feel proud that Edward Lhuyd listed the flora of Snowdon on a visit to the mountain in 1688, where he identified this lovely flower, first named after him: Lloydia serotina.

There are special invertebrates too. A few examples of a species of rainbow beetle, the genetically distinct Chrysolina cerealis, the Snowdon rainbow beetle, were trapped, like the Snowdon lily, after the last Ice Age. The creature survived to evolve alone on Snowdon's western flanks, on crags away from grazing sheep. It feeds on flowers of the wild thyme. Even its breakfast sounds romantic!

The climb takes all the energy of body and mind, and only the naturalist knows where to look for a tiny flower or a beetle. When you walk a mountain track, stepping up, up the shale paths, stopping to catch your breath, to gaze into rain, or mist, or sometimes across infinite space to far peaks and valleys rising at every upward step, the voids beneath your feet, and the dead who hollowed them, can be far from mind. One is the opposite of the other, as light is of the dark, as airy space is of claustrophobic enclosure. Yet the spent power of the pits and quarries has left behind volumes of emptiness, and water. The mountain strums with rivers, lakes and waterfalls, sings with streams, Glaslyn, Gorsen, Cwm Llan, Afon y Cwm. There are ruins of farms, the *hafod* (the shepherd's summer house), and the *hendr*e (his winter house), quarrymen's sleeping barracks, bridges and walls made of slate, rubble, and river stones. Ghost-works rust and rattle in the wind, dead streams blue with copper, deserted mine works, cathedrals of emptiness where it is impossible to forget the people who lived briefly and died there.

Without subsistence farming there would not have been slate. Without slate, there would be no farms up here, in this windswept place. The ruins of both are the story. Men came from the hill-farms of greater Snowdonia, or as far afield as Anglesey, leaving behind a bit of land to work, a large family to feed. Father and older brothers travelled to work six days a week in the quarry or the mine, while mother and daughters cared for stock, and tilled a scrape of land.

The mountain has secrets,
tunnels into the seep and drip of the dark,
into the stone womb, under roots of trees,
past wheels, pulleys, chains, trucks locked
in their pollens of rust.

Deep as the Ordovician, old workings,
mine-shafts, mullock heaps, piles of slag,
abandoned two centuries back, river-stones
stained blue with copper, copper-iron's gold,
sulphates from the mountain's heart.

Imagine the miner stoop under its porch,
to the knees in ice where light dies at the brink.
Darkness. Echoes. Bats hang like rags. A stream
falls three hundred feet in glittering stillness,
and ferns sip sunlight at a rock fissure.

Rungs crook rusted steps over the void,
the miner's footprint in air, his handprint on rock
slimed by centuries of rain. He and water
hollowed the mountain, the falling stone
of his cry swallowed in centuries of silence.

Once, after a long climb in a company of poets, we stoop into the mountain past No Entry, *Perygl*, Danger, beneath a low portal in sheer rock. We follow an arrow of torchlight, stepping along rusted tramlines into a black tunnel, narrow and low at first, before space opens suddenly, vertiginously into the first gallery. We know the void without seeing anything but blackness. It is measured in the altered note of our breaths, heartbeats, voices. It hears our bodies' vibrations sounding a pit too vast for the beam of a torch to measure. It has its own sounds too. There are cries and whispers out there, down there, in the void. Our eyes get used to the dark. First a streak of gold light from the roof of the mine – a stream falling through a rock fissure, sleeved in fern, then water falling free through light into dark. Someone with a powerful flashlight sends a beam to touch the far wall. We make out hooks and rungs driven into the rock where miners climbed all day long, slept seven nights in slate barracks on the mountain, worked the face for six days, went home for Sunday chapel, a few family hours, then returned to work their youth and health away. Many fell from those hooks and rungs into the terrible void below. To oblivion. Imagine the curved sound diminishing into the depths where a man's cry drowns but never stops echoing.

Not just slate, but copper, and other metals and minerals were worked from these mountains, left hollow and haunted once the profits were made. The life of a falling miner was soon replaced from the endless queue of the jobless, trying to add to the income of subsistence farming. Departed profiteers leave nothing behind but ghosts.

Slate is slow in the making. It is the finest-grained of all rock. Foliated, metamorphic, formed in a furnace of low heat and pressure out of sedimentary shale that had already been laid down millions of years earlier as clay or volcanic ash. Thought of those ages makes me dizzy, aeons of volcanic activity, the rise and fall of oceans, pressure of sedimentary leftovers, glaciers and their detritus. The mineral recipe is geology's music: quartz, muscovite, illite, biotite, chlorite, hematite, pyrite, sometimes apatite, graphite, kaolinite, magnetite, tourmaline, zircon, feldspar. Sometimes there are iron nuclei in Snowdonian slate, forming 'bubbles' of pale green in the purple. I step across such a threshold every day. Sometimes there are the remains of delicate organisms.

The foliation of slate can lie vertical to the direction of the compression. A skilled slate cutter can split slates clean and flat and of a size ready for roofing, or thick ones for flooring, larger for gravestones, fences, stiles, a massive slab for a dairy or larder. We have always found uses for the power of water inside or on the mountain. I think of the simple way they churned butter in my mother's home farm. Hand-churning butter is hard work, and there were ten children in the family. Opposite the farm door there was a gap in the wall high above a fast-flowing stream. The churn was placed in the gap, and connected to a small waterwheel turned by the current in the river below. Thus every day milk was churned to fresh butter. A few hundred yards downstream the same millstream ground the corn for flour. The power of water is infinite and its uses multiple. It is never exhausted.

The rise and fall of demand, and storage of unused power, are still unsolved problems in the generation and use of electricity. We must generate for maximum demand, and waste the rest. One of Britain's most impressive electricity power stations is at the abandoned Dinorwic slate quarry, its machinery buried deep inside the mountain, Elidir Fawr. Water is stored high above in the Marchlyn reservoir. At times of peak demand, the gates are opened and water is set free to pour down, down through the turbines into Llyn Peris. At night, times of low demand, the water is pumped back up into the reservoir, and held until needed. Power withheld. Its metaphor might be the two mythical dragons of Snowdon, whose final battle gave victory to the red dragon over the white. I think of that sleeping power when, on a clear day, I see the blue peak of Snowdon, unmistakable across the waters of Cardigan Bay.

Snowdon's main farm, Hafod y Llan, the mountain grazing, its rivers and lakes, are now run by the National Trust, saved from the mad, bad dreams of a developer with a hotel, powerboats and lakeside development in mind. Instead, the mountain flock is limited to one thousand sheep, the grazing and house are run organically, and the Trust has developed a new hydroelectricity scheme. A turbine beside broken walls in the copper-poisoned waters of Craflwyn, 'dead' blue-green waters where no fish live, now produces enough electricity for all the National Trust's houses in Wales. What has been ripped from the guts of the mountain, scattering the slopes with ruins and the bones of the dead, impoverished a tenant people and enriched distant landowners, has found a kind of resolution. Hafod y Llan is ours, and Eryri awaits the return of the eagles.

SOMETHING UNDERSTOOD

A team of roadmen was working the lanes of Banc Sion Cwilt, a local name for the small patch of high land where we live. One of the men was described by his fellow workmen as 'simple'. He believed the earth to be flat. The roadmen teased him. 'What's over the horizon then, Dai?' He replied, 'A ditch. With workmen making stars out of old moons.'

Was he simple? Or a poet, wiser than they knew, making myth from mystery? We live in a dark place. There are no street lights. To the west is the sea, to the east, hill country hides the lights of villages, to south and north no light stains the sky. The trig point behind our house records the hill rising to a thousand feet.

At One Thousand Feet[1]

Nobody comes but the postman
and the farmer with winter fodder.
A-road and motorway avoid me.
The national grid has left me out.
For power I catch wind.
In my garden clear water rises.
A wind spinning the blades
of the mill to blinding silver
lets in the rumour,
grief on the radio.

---

1 'At One Thousand Feet' (*Collected Poems*).

America telephones.
A postcard comes from Poland.
In the sling of its speed the comet
flowers to perihelion over the chimney.
I hold the sky to my ear to hear
pandemonium whispering.

Now we are now connected to the national grid, and our turbine, too small for our needs, has gone, but before its removal a roadman asked was it permitted by the electricity company. 'Aren't you stealing their wind?' he said.

Stealing the wind! We have evolved to think in poetry; all human beings are poets; poetry distinguishes the human animal from other living creatures; poetry – as epic, lyric, song, narrative, myth, in formal or free verse – is the truth, wider, deeper, more nuanced than plain fact. It is through poetry that we explain the inexplicable. Poetry is a rhythmic way of thinking, the heartbeat of human thought, reason and imagination. Metaphor is our way of reading the mysteries of the universe. What we don't understand – in art, science, technology, engineering, mathematics, religion, philosophy – we explain to ourselves in metaphor. The internet uses metaphor to describe itself. The 'mouse' moves under my right hand. We 'travel' the 'web'. Radio's few minutes of 'wild sound' record the right atmosphere of silence before recording a programme. A television cameraman complains of 'a hare (hair) in the gate'. Architects call tracks worn by human feet across landscaped areas around buildings 'paths of desire'. The poet R.S. Thomas, explaining his belief in God, spoke of putting his hand in the empty form of a hare, and finding it warm, like a room someone had just left. One offence committed in a game of rugby, tackling, lifting and dropping an opponent, is called a 'spear'.

I was once teaching a workshop on metaphor to primary school children, though *they* thought we were just writing a group poem about a tree. I asked them what a tree was *like*. Like a hand, said one child. I asked for words connected with hands. 'What do hands do?' I asked, and wrote down what they said. Hands wave, write, stroke. At last, I confessed I'd played a trick, and read their poem back to them, the word 'tree' replacing 'hand'. When I read aloud the line, 'The tree writes on the sky', up jumped the least able boy – the naughty one, the slow reader, the one who was threatened by his teacher, behave or you're out. He stood up, his two hands in the air, shouting, 'YES! I get it! Hand! Tree!' It was 'something understood'.

We look up at the night sky, and we map it for the shapes we see, the Square of Pegasus, the Plough, Orion, named for the gods who ride their chariots up there, who shake the heavens with lightning, who send an occasional comet to remind us of our subordinate place in the order of things, who cause floods, earthquakes, hurricanes to warn us we are killing the planet. The ancient naming and its mythology endure. We have written our human story on the sky's page.

Once, in the 1980s at Tŷ Newydd, our Welsh Writers' house, I tutored a poetry course for sixteen-year-olds from Reading. One clear night we doused the house lights and stepped out to watch the Perseids, the August meteor shower. We lay on our backs on the lawn. Between their chorus of cries at every shooting star, I pointed out the planets, the constellations, the Milky Way. The students were astonished. For them such heavenly bodies belonged in science fiction comics and movies. Suddenly, one of the boys uttered these immortal words:

> 'Wow! Do we 'ave these in Reading?'

Has wonder been lost? Do we think we have solved the last mystery, found the final piece of the jigsaw, the God particle? Are wonder, and worship, no more? Could it be that, in the blind heavens of Reading, and every neon-lit city, town, village in the whole world, the night sky is available only on television?

My key words are wonder, worship, and story. I'm not talking about religion, certainly not theology, absolutely not dogma. Wonder is what our ancestors felt, worship arose from it, and story was how they explained the inexplicable to themselves. It is no surprise to know that our ancestors worshipped the heavens and the earth, and that we are inclined not to worship anything. Yet we do feel wonder, don't we? Wonder is a questing, questioning word. Its manifestation is a kind of worship, an urge to follow the thrill of wonder by wanting to save the planet. R.S. Thomas, our, great, late Welsh poet, a priest himself, wrote in his poem, 'The Moor':

'It was like a church to me.'[1]

In her memoir, *Pilgrim at Tinker Creek*, Annie Dillard, poet and poetic writer of prose, describes seeing a mockingbird drop like a stone from the top of a four-storey building, to open its wings a breath before reaching the ground. Another time she saw green waves roll ashore off Florida, translucent and backlit by the sun, carrying the twisting bodies of shark. 'The least we can do,' she writes, 'is try to be there.'

We have evidence that our early ancestors were as watchful of the sky above them as they were of the earth they walked on. Observation of the moon and stars, of sunrise and sunset, the change of seasons, the weather, were all they knew of science, and of worship. *Brut y Tywysogion*, or 'The

---

1 'The Moor', R.S. Thomas.

Chronicle of the Princes', recorded that between 685 and 691, 'the earth quaked in Brittany', 'there was a rain of blood in the island of Britain and Ireland.' 'The butter and the milk turned to blood.' 'And the moon was blood.' Those events were understood as warnings.

These nights, as we move towards winter, we look out for Jupiter, stepping along the planet-road, flanked by his moons, four of them clearly discernible through our telescope in the dark skies over this hill, locally known as Banc Sion Cwilt. Sion was a smuggler working the coast close to where we live. He wore a coloured quilt for a coat. The place he haunted is named for him, as we name the planets in the dark sky above us. To name them is to possess them, to make them part of our world and our story. As Shakespeare says in *A Midsummer Night's Dream*:

The poet's eye, in a fine frenzy rolling,
Doth glance from heaven to earth, from earth to heaven;
And as imagination bodies forth
The forms of things unknown, the poet's pen
Turns them to shapes and gives to airy nothing
A local habitation and a name.

My Iron Age ancestors could calculate, measure and predict the length of the day, the angle of the sun, the waning and waxing of the moon, seasonal changes. The mathematics of observation. When my son was six he made a sundial on the lawn:

In the still
Centre he pushed the broken bean
Stick, gathering twelve fragments
Of stone. Placed them at measured
Distances. Then he crouched, slightly

Trembling with fever, calculating
The mathematics of sunshine.

He was trying to tell the time from sunlight and shadow, as people did five thousand years ago, when they built passage graves such as Newgrange in Ireland. At dawn after the longest night of the year, a cunning slit left above the portal by those ancient builders lets in a spear of light which reaches deep into the passage to touch the great stone. Their building was constructed to a precise calculation. After the darkness, the cold, the sterility of winter, the ray of sunlight touching the stone at sunrise on the shortest day of the year symbolises a wakening, a quickening, an insemination of the earth itself, urged awake after winter sleep. All along the Atlantic coast the remains of these powerful buildings are evidence of human reason and calculation at work together with worship in the culture of our ancestors. Plant pollens have been found in some of the oldest burial sites on earth, telling us that, faced with the mystery of death and grief, they were human as we are. We 'glance from heaven to earth, from earth to heaven'. Then something else happens:

imagination bodies forth
The forms of things unknown, the poet's pen
Turns them to shapes and gives to airy nothing
A local habitation and a name.

Poetry is our narrative, and at the heart of the telling is repetition. Story has always been crucial to our understanding of 'life, the universe and everything', of heaven and earth. How else to explain the sun, the moon, the extreme weathers of storm, thunder, flood, hurricane, earthquake, darkness and light. The gods were angry, or pleased. The moon was blood. Early humans explained the great, omnificent gold sun by calling it a god. We know it is a star, but that does not erase from our minds, our literature, our music, our culture the memory and naming of the gods. On the contrary, it leaves an extra shade of meaning, and to this day stories are the means by which we fathom the unfathomable. Early poetry, like poetry today, uses rhythm, repetition and metaphor to help us memorise, to explain things simply to ourselves and to each other. 'Grandma's gone to heaven,' we tell a child. It is not a lie. It is a metaphor, because the truth is we don't know where she's gone. How can the dead live in us still, as they do, if they are nothing but bones in the ground, or ashes blown away on the wind? Only metaphor comes to our rescue at such a moment.

It is easy to imagine the narrative epic, sung, maybe, to the harp, passed from speaker to listeners round a fire under the stars, maybe chanted, repeated to each other and to the gods. 'Song' and 'poem' both lie in the Welsh words *cân* and *cerdd*. In English too, a particular kind of poem, the lyric, suggests the words of a song, and the epic suggests story. The stories we tell ourselves allow us to escape the trap of literalism, and, that most unattractive human characteristic, certainty, the 'I am right' of the doctrinal zealot. The verse narrative tells the human story with imagination, not dogma.

The oldest stories we know, and the earliest art, show that human beings used the moon and the sun for their calculations. To 'worship' is human. It recognises Earth's mysterious relationship with sun and moon, stars and planets, seasons and the weather, and of our subordinate place in it. No wonder they felt the need to appease the gods. We know, and they knew, that if we hurt the planet, we die. How could we not gaze at the heavens? The first humans saw the shadow edge across the moon, a little more each night, the sun rise every day, shortening and lengthening days, and lived by their light. I watched a complete eclipse of the moon as it slowly lost first its edge then its brilliance. In eclipse it was just a stone. No longer a goddess, but a sad stone, looking close and ordinary enough to pluck from the sky, the more moving for being just a pebble. Then I thought – that's our shadow, Earth's shadow that has put out its light. This metaphor for our carelessness reminded me of three old men I saw sitting on a bench in the sun. A white moth fluttered close to them. One of them, without pausing his talk, caught and crushed it in his fist.

Eclipse of the Moon[1]

Whose shadow's that?
Who walked in the evening
at his own ghost's back?
Who trod in the circle,
left a footprint on the frozen pond?
Who looked in the mirror
and clouded the glass?
Who snatched the white moth
in his closed fist?
Who drowned
reaching for the coin?

Around 600 B.C. an anonymous Chinese poet says, on seeing the new moon rise over the hill, 'my heart lays down its load'. A thousand years later, in Arthur Waley's translation of Yang-Ti, we read, of the same moon,

Suddenly a wave carries the moon away
And the tidal water comes with its freight of stars.

Milton describes Lucifer, once the brightest of all the angels, after his fall from grace:

---

1 'Eclipse of the Moon', *Collected Poems.*

as when the sun, new-risen,
Looks through the horizontal misty air
Shorn of his beams

We talk of the man in the moon. In parts of Africa it is the hare in the moon. It is more than a stone. The moon by which we measure months and years, inspires, rules, female in our culture, male in others, goddess, god, praised by poets from ancient times to today in every culture, shone down on Juliet and her Romeo. Close by as I write, is a hare carved from limestone by the sculptor, Meic Watts. I see moonlit, shallow, ancient seas when the stone from which the hare is made was still forming in what we now call Derbyshire, before a human foot had trod the earth. I imagine the physical earth in formation, the moon before we mythologised it, before we were here to dream the gods, or sculpt a hare from stone. My sonnet is a song for art and science.

The Stone Hare[2]

Think of it waiting three hundred million years,
not a hare hiding in the last stand of wheat,
but a premonition of stone, a moonlit reef
where corals reach for the light through clear
waters of warm Palaeozoic seas.
In its limbs lies the story of the earth,
the living ocean, then the slow birth
of limestone from the long trajectories
of starfish, feather stars, crinoids and crushed shells
that fill with calcite, harden, wait for the quarryman,
the timed explosion and the sculptor's hand.
Then the hare, its eye a planet, springs from the chisel

2 'The Stone Hare', *Collected Poems*.

to stand in the grass, moonlight's muscle and bone,
the stems of sea lilies slowly turned to stone.

George Herbert's sonnet 'Prayer' is a meditation, but Herbert was a poet, and he concludes with two words that are the best definition of poetry I know:

Prayer, the Church's banquet, Angels' age,
God's breath in man returning to his birth,
The soul in paraphrase, heart in pilgrimage,
The Christian plummet sounding heav'n and earth;
Engine against th' Almighty, sinner's tower,
Reversed thunder, Christ-side-piercing spear,
The six-days'-world transposing in an hour,
A kind of tune, which all things hear and fear;
Softness, and peace, and joy, and love, and bliss,
Exalted manna, gladness of the best,
Heaven in ordinary, man well dressed,
The milky way, the bird of Paradise,
Church bells beyond the stars heard, the soul's blood,
The land of spices, something understood.

DYLAN THOMAS: MUSIC AND TRUTH

'The Sound and Shape of Carmarthen Bay'

In the summer of Dylan's centenary year, a mare called Leila leaned into her harness and pulled a covered wagon weighted with literary pilgrims through sunlit Carmarthenshire lanes, to visit Fern Hill, Waunfwlchan, Blaen Cwm, Llanybri, Laugharne, places redolent with the poet's words. Leila's hoof-beats rhymed the day. When the lane narrowed, thorny wands lashed the wagon's open sides, and lashed us too, as Dylan describes in 'The Peaches'.

Dylan Thomas is one of the twentieth century's great poets. His work endures. Many of his lines and images are part of our thinking. He shares with James Joyce two powerful qualities: music and truth. He made language new. He woke us with his witty, wild way with words. It is no coincidence that he arrived as the popularity of radio surged. He was soon discovered by BBC Radio Wales, then called the Welsh Home Service, who commissioned and broadcast a remarkable series of talks, stories, and his 'play for voices', *Under Milk Wood.* His voice became familiar to listeners, his poetry popular. When we speak of 'the poet's voice', we mean the recognisable written style of a particular poet, but Dylan's 'voice', in the poems, stories, prose, verse drama, unmistakable as it rises from the silence of the page, was, in his case, also familiar as a sound.

I want to focus on two of his best-known poems, and one short story, on their special qualities of music and truth. Poetry sang in all that he wrote. His use of English was the sound of his early world, and of his true experience – not cold fact, but lived truth to what he knew, heard, breathed as child, youth, young man. His words are first words. He spent years in London, New York, and elsewhere, scriptwriting, talking, lecturing, performing his work, but it was at home in West Wales, Laugharne, New Quay, in sight of the 'fishing-boat bobbing sea' that he wrote his poetry. For Dylan, Swansea, Carmarthenshire and Ceredigion were where language began, where it entered him, heart, soul and senses, where the word became flesh.

His poems came slowly. Many were decades in the making. Almost every poem grew from an idea scrawled in teenage notebooks in his box-bedroom at 5 Cwmdonkin Drive, Swansea, where he read Shakespeare, Gerard Manley Hopkins, and the books his grammar-school English-teacher father gave him, and where the seed was sown for some of his finest poems. He explained that, when outside Wales, he could remember superficial details, such as 'settles in the corners, hams on the hooks', but that he found it harder to remember what birds sounded like and said in Gower, and what sort of a 'sound and shape was Carmarthen Bay'.

His alertness to lived truth, to word and world made flesh, gives all his work, however wildly imaginative – poems, stories, articles, autobiographical pieces – the raw heat of experience which few writers reach. When a writer gives us the perfect image, we trust it. The mind shouts 'Yes!' I wish I had been first to hear 'speeches' in the sound of water, in tap, cistern or stream, to see bones as like lilies, or note 'the heron-priested shore', where tall, still, cleric-like birds keep an eye out for fish in the Tywi estuary, as the train pulls out of Carmarthen.

Truth wins, and style takes care of itself in Dylan's work, as it does in the writings of Joyce, and of a few others, accurate listeners who found poetry in the authentic sound around them. That alertness of body and mind to the world and the ability to record and tell it true is remarkable, and thrilling to read. Lesser writers observe, a little apart, then reach for the thesaurus, for other writers' observations, for the expected details, 'the settle in the corner, the hams on the hooks'.

In his powerful story, 'The Peaches', on the first day of the holidays schoolboy Dylan rides in the cart beside his drunken Uncle to Fern Hill – Gorsehill in the story – 'the lilting house' where on arrival, spooked by the dark yard, he bolts into Auntie Annie's arms. Uncle Jim, Fern Hill's tenant farmer, stole piglets from the sow to pay for his pleasures in 'The Hare's Foot', or 'The Pure Drop', after market day in Carmarthen, as told in Dylan's story.

His best friend, Jack Williams, arrives to join him next day for a fortnight's holiday, brought by his rich mother in a Daimler. Annie gets things wrong: her welcome, her shoes, a tin of peaches. Mrs Williams sneers and departs. Annie is humiliated. Despite this, the boys spend a joyful evening playing Indians in the wilderness around the farm, and Dylan vividly remembers and describes how his whole boy-body and mind were alive in the joy of the game.

But that night, from their room above the kitchen, the boys overhear Uncle Jim ranting about Mrs Williams 'with her bloody motor car and her bloody son'. So the game of Indians is over. The summer holiday that began in joy ends in heartbreak. Jack leaves the next day.

Yet, it was there, at Fern Hill, 'the lilting house', where Dylan was young, that time held him 'green and dying'. The farmhouse is today a faded Georgian house behind padlocked gates. Yet to the boy Dylan, it was 'lovely', it was 'green and golden', and he was young, carefree, green, alive, the more green, the more alive for his awareness of death. He is telling it true.

A second special quality which I identify in great writing, in poetry or prose, is music: the sound that sings on in the reader's mind, the lilting line or the lovely language of syntax. Along with owls, 'bearing the farm away' in 'Fern Hill', cockerels, one always on the farm's shoulder, and herons, 'the heron-priested shore' of 'Poem in October', horses are Dylan's beasts of yard and field, as china dogs and stuffed foxes are his parlour creatures. The poet's work is full of horses, and carts, 'flashing into the dark' in his Prologue to the poems. The horse was the key memory for those who made the centenary pilgrimage to Fern Hill, and, as hoof-beats were the iambics of the Carmarthenshire countryside that day, so the imagery and rhythm of horses are at work in many of Dylan's poems and stories set on the family farms of his childhood in rural Carmarthenshire.

Dylan is poetry's song thrush, above all a poet of word-music. Take the villanelle, a form often killed as a creative-writing class exercise. In my opinion possibly the finest villanelle ever written is Dylan's lament as he watches at his father's deathbed: 'Do not go gentle into that good night'. It is a real poem, a cry of pain which uses the form like hurt skin. In keeping with formal rules, the key lines repeat, but each time he repeats a line Dylan manages a subtle change of grammar, meaning and stress. Thus, in line one, verse one, 'Do not go gentle', and the second line that begins, 'Rage, rage', are imperatives, commands to his dying father, 'Do not go', and then to all the dying to 'Rage, rage' before the lights go out. In verse two, 'do not' is a simple verb, the verb's subject, grammatically, being 'wise men'. Likewise in verse three, 'rage, rage' is a simple verb, repeated. And so it moves, syntactically shifting emphases. We read the lines differently each time, so we hear new meaning with each reprise. Few villanelles achieve this. It is a beautiful poem fired by grief, shaped by but freed from the form.

Then there's the *sound* of it. The pentameter of the first line echoes the rhythm of horse and cart on a country lane, a familiar, remembered sound to schoolboy Dylan in his box-bedroom in Cwmdonkin Drive, reading his Shakespeare, writing poems, remembering hoof-beats on the lanes to Fern Hill. The rhythm of a horse's hooves heard in his childhood beats in this lament for his dying father. He writes of time as if then and now, a radiant past and a grieving present, were one, lost joy recalled, the more luminous for death's shadow. Dylan's greatest poems are both 'green and dying', at once lit by childhood joy and darkened by its loss.

Dylan did not speak Welsh, but he heard it, he knew it. As a poet, his language arose from that commonly spoken about him, and was influenced by the fine Welsh of his poet-preacher relatives, one of them a famous *prifardd*, a chaired eisteddfod poet. That day as we rode the lanes my fellow poet guide, T. James Jones, 'Jim Parc Nest', former Archdruid, noted that the first, repeated line is a perfect example of *cynghanedd*. There is not time here to speak in detail about the sound-patterns of *cynghanedd*, described in the *Princeton Encyclopedia of Poetry and Poetics* as 'the most sophisticated poetics in the world', but, sure enough, the opening consonants, d,n,t,g (do not go, pronounced as a child would say them) are echoed, in reverse, by the g,d,n,t (goodnight), that close the line. What counts in *cynghanedd* is what we hear, not what we see, and 'd' and 't' are interchangeable. His use of *cynghanedd* is no accident. Dylan heard Welsh spoken at Fern Hill, sung in Smyrna chapel, recited at eisteddfodau. It is the tongue of 'the lilting house', the barns, the happy yard.

Dylan's prose is written with a poet's flow and sound. His word choice, 'lovely', for example, must be heard in the context of his perfect ear for how his people spoke. We should not hear 'lovely' as too ordinary an adjective, but as an honest south-west Wales word, as 'my lovely', often used to address a complete stranger, two syllables common and repetitive as blackbird song. Some complain that its use twice, and so close together, in verse three of 'Fern Hill' is a weakness. But it is his truth, the word choice and accent of place, and we believe it. Not for him the thesaurus, particularly in a poem like 'Fern Hill' where he remembers and records the precise sound and shape of that place, that time. 'Green' is used six times in 'Fern Hill', pealing like a bell throughout the poem. It is the colour of life while time held him 'green and dying'.

'Lovely', 'wicked', 'tidy', ordinary words used strangely and locally in south-west Wales, ring in *Under Milk Wood*, his heartbreakingly funny, poetic radio play for voices, written in New Quay, in sight and sound of Cardigan Bay. Script-writer, broadcaster, performer, he was alert to every beat of the language he had heard around him since the day he was born. Dylan's parents' roots were in rural Carmarthenshire, as were those of my own paternal family. His family, like mine, were mostly respectable, chapel-going, Welsh-speaking, 'tidy' country people. There is a wide sea of difference between 'tidy', and 'rough', words much used by his people, and by mine. Such people minded about a well-scrubbed doorstep, chapel on Sundays, a proper cooked dinner, a clean cloth on the table. Welsh was the family language, until Dylan's grammar-school teacher-father chose English, and elocution lessons, for his son – an effort to move up a notch and be more than 'tidy'. When Dylan's parents moved into a modest Swansea suburb, the farmhouse objects, 'the knitted text, "Prepare to Meet thy God", the grandmother clock, the smiling china dogs', survived as relics. In Dylan's notebook, dated 1930–32, there is a little note of desperation, scrawled in his box-bedroom in Cwmdonkin Drive: '(Oh change the life!, The sideboard fruit, the ferns, the picture houses. And the pack of cards.)' Downstairs a sideboard had by then replaced the dresser, a pack of cards the knitted text. The ferns remain.

In the sunlit lane at 'Fern Hill', we pilgrims heard what he had heard – the lane where 'time' let the poet-boy hail the horse-drawn wagon to stop and let him climb the 'house-high hay' and ride home, 'prince of the apple towns'. We heard too, from the other Fern Hill, Gorsehill of 'The Peaches', the ring of cobbles, the 'hollowed' stables, the farmhouse stairs, each one with a 'different voice'. We clip-clopped through 'the parables of sunlight' of his far away childhood and our present, past Waunfwlchan, Blaen Cwm, at last leaving Leila and the trap for the bus to Penycoed, the churchyard at Llanybri, Annie's grave, to Laugharne and Browns Hotel, and the Boathouse on its 'breakneck of rocks', where waves are horses.

Dylan Thomas had perfect pitch for the music of being human, and the rhythms of Welsh, that other drum, retune his English for a new poetry. This music, this truth, voices the true 'sound and shape of Carmarthen Bay', and the place speaks it still: the tidy wives, the mussel-pickers, the heron-priested shore. 'Fern Hill' sings aloud his unique genius. His obsession with 'time' brings the sensuous, sunlit dreamworld of childhood into the darkness of now and turns it to song, and the poem's closing lines psalm shape and sound, truth and music, life and death, green and dying, how it 'sang in its chains, like the sea'.

RETURN TO COLD KNAP LAKE

Poems wait wordless for their moment to be written. Or almost wordless. They can lie quietly in wait for poetry's attention for weeks, years, or a lifetime, in 'the rag-and-bone-shop of the heart'.[1]

For me 'Cold Knap Lake' is one such poem, along with many others that have their source in that time, that place, kept safe in the rich compost heap of memory. When I was a year old, my parents moved to our first family house: 'Flatholm', named after one of the two islands, Flat Holm and Steep Holm, which we could see out in the Bristol Channel from the beach nearby. My bedroom window overlooked the lake in the park just across the road from our house. 'Cold Knap' was the third line in my childhood home address: Flatholm, Lakeside, Cold Knap, Barry, Glamorgan. We lived there until I was ten, crucial years in the development of a child's memory and imagination, a time of deepening and accumulating language, of imbibing stories, nursery rhymes, myths and legends, of exploring a gradually widening geography of the outdoor world of the street, and, in my case, of the park, the woods, cliffs and beaches.

I loved the name: Cold Knap Lake. I liked the beat of those three one-syllable words, especially the word Knap, the Old English word for hillock, or headland. The Knap was named for the promontory jutting into the Bristol Channel between two beaches, maybe half a mile south of the harp-shaped lake in the park where I and gangs of children played

1 W.B. Yeats.

throughout childhood. But why 'cold'? I don't know, but the word adds to its allure, holding within the image the snowy winters I remember from childhood, especially the legendary snow and ice of 1941 and 1947. There were often accidents in the park, cuts, broken bones and, in the lake and in the outdoor swimming pool nearby or the sea not half a mile away, people in trouble, drunks, drownings and almost-drownings. There was an American airbase not far away, and the park and roads were still unlit in the closing years of the 1939–45 war. Drunken airmen tottering back to camp often fell into the lake's feeder ponds. My mother, a trained nurse, kept her first aid box by the front door.

The poem recalls, as accurately as possible, an occasion when a man knocked on our front door and called for my mother to give first aid to a child who had been pulled from the lake, apparently lifeless. I was about seven or eight years old. The child was four or five. She lay on the shore where people had placed her, draped with waterweed, 'water's long green silk'. I stood with the crowd of people watching from a few yards away while my mother gave the child artificial respiration, that we know as 'the kiss of life'. My mother was a beauty, with red, Pre-Raphaelite curls, and, as a cherished child and too adventurous for my own good, I knew she could kiss people better like no other. I watched her, misunderstanding the medical emergency procedure, but entranced, trusting, scared, and proud.

The lake is memory, as places such as castles and ancient earthworks are history, the personal and impersonal versions of the past. Water has special qualities which make it a good metaphor for memory. I have a notion that everything that has ever happened at a lake is stored twice in the water – in the reflective surface and in the murky depths. The lake 'remembers' faces and skies in its mirror surface, and in the thrown coins, lost watches, lockets and wedding rings in its impenetrable muddy depths. And events are kept safe a third way in the memory of anyone who happened to be there. Places 'remember' for us. Remind us. Children sometimes turn verb and subject round, and use the word 'remembers' in a way that suggests that it is the inanimate thing, event or place that has a memory. The place where we saw a runaway horse 'remembers', or where we picnicked once, lost a favourite toy, where we quarrelled, or fell in love.

Water reflects. The mind reflects. Still water is a good metaphor for memory, and for the past. That almost-drowning, that stretch of water, had double power for the nascent poet in me from the start, but gained even more by echoing detail from the Welsh myths my father told me, the fairy stories my mother read to me, and which, by the time I was four or five, I was reading for myself, over and over, obsessed. In those stories, children were entrapped by an Ice Queen, or stepped through a looking glass, were carried away by swans, taken by the sea-god to his watery kingdom and turned into seagulls to return to shore every evening to meet their father when he called their names. I was stolen away and taken to the kingdom under the sea, Daddy on the shore, calling my name. There were paintings too: in my Arthur Mee's *Children's Encyclopedia* was a picture by the Pre-Raphaelite painter, Millais, of Ophelia floating among flowers strewn in a stream. As a child, I loved that picture. I was unafraid of water and never remember not being able to swim. I was so confident in water that I liked to float on my back, like Ophelia in the painting, not drowning but dreamily floating, my arms slack, like sleeping in a calm sea or pool. A small arm movement, a flick of fins or a mermaid's tail, would propel me through the water.

That there might be a connection between the girl in my poem and the Millais painting of Ophelia only occurred to me long after the poem was written, by which time I had also seen many staged productions of *Hamlet*. However, it was far from my conscious mind when I wrote the poem. Likewise, my memory preceded by decades my reading of the poetry of W.B. Yeats, and his many references to swans. I, the poet, went way back into memory, past *Hamlet* and his tragedy, past all grown-up literature, to the child I had been, haunted by nursery rhymes and fairy stories. In writing I concentrated only on remembering the child who fell into the lake and nearly drowned while reaching for a stick, but was saved by my mother's kiss.

To the bookish child I was, stories were as real as life, and from babyhood I took in the songs, word-music and rhythms of nursery rhymes. So, by the time I, the adult, wrote the poem, though speaking through my childhood self, I had read, among many other swan poems, Yeats's 'The Wild Swans at Coole'. The very word 'swan' will have called Yeats's swans to mind, whether I knew it or not, as well as the swans on the shore of Cold Knap Lake, together with every swan ever encountered in literature or life. Every word – swan, lake, cold, water – bears its load. That is why language is such a potent possession. When I say 'swan', I am using one of the first words I knew. I return to where all poets source their words: the beginning of language. Water. Swan. Baby. Duck. Lake. Girl.

My work is not fiction. Poetry is the truth. The poem recounts the story of the girl in the lake as accurately as I could make it, recalling what I saw that childhood day, until the last two lines of verse three, where there is a change. Then I tell not what I witnessed, but what I overheard my father tell my mother. The poem takes a turn as my father takes up the narrative, and I am an eavesdropper, his words not intended for my ears. What he said frightened me, as most fairy stories did. I feel a moment of doubt, and verse four begins with the question: 'Was I there?' But I *was* there, by the lake when it happened, and in the house, hearing my father tell his part of the story. The first verses were observation, but this was overheard, me listening, not seeing, and the slight distancing from events makes space for Grimm's and other alarming fairy stories to enter the poem. The unreal world of the myth is even more frightening than real life. Until the moment, in verse three, lines three and four, when I report my father's words, and the myths take over, I am sure of the accuracy of every detail. Then I hear him tell my mother that the child was 'thrashed for almost drowning'. I, the adult poet, have always excused the distraught parents for that moment's violence, but the child in me was afraid, and from that moment the poem takes a dark turn, I am no longer safe. The most frightening fairy stories carry us into dark worlds, in imagination and in the poem. I don't take a deliberate turn. The words carry me there.

The change lets nursery rhyme influence the poem's music. Again, this is not a conscious move. Poets listen for language, and I like to let it come naturally. The double-rhyming couplet that closes the poem had come into my mind unbidden. Once those lines were written, I returned to the early verses to work on half-rhymes all the way through the poem in second, third, fourth or more drafts. I wanted no more than an echo between the end-words of the earlier lines, just a repeated end-of-word, end-of-line consonant, and nothing forced. The final couplet had come as easily as if the pen found it on the page, rhyming two of my favourite words: water and daughter. It is part of the rhyme-pleasure that their spelling is at odds with their pronunciation, and, with the eccentricity of English pronunciation, they rhyme in spite of their appearance. 'Daughter' with 'water', not with 'laughter', as 'water' does not rhyme with 'later'.

The events are clear to this day, remembered by the child I was, still alive inside me, the child who knew nothing of death other than the deaths of pets, of farm animals, and news of distant relatives; nothing of despair, nothing of unhappy endings, except the death of Lassie, the collie in the film. (I recall having to reread the story of Babar the Elephant to my daughter with a changed ending, because she was too upset to bear hearing it again as it was.) The mature poet dips a pen into memory, and tells the child's story, but by now that story is influenced by a lifetime of education, reading, hearing music, being alive, being aware, suddenly, of 'that troubled surface' which the pen finds as it sounds the mind, finds words, and uncurls from the pen onto the page. It feels like chance, swift and instinctive, and it is important that it should be so. The pen *finds* the words. R.S. Thomas spoke of 'taking pen and paper to see what words will do'. Students ask me, 'What were your feelings?' or 'What were you thinking?' I answer, I don't know. But I know that the word 'bleating' came to mind from my experience of my grandparents' farms, and of delivering lambs myself. The lamb, born from the birth-flood, like the child delivered from the lake, takes its first breath, and bleats. It is a joyful sound. It's the sound of life. The pen drew that word from my life.

To speak plainly, in spite of the Millais painting (happily misread by me, the child, as a picture of dreamy floating), the poem is *not* about suicide, as has been suggested by some teachers. Five-year-old children do not want to die. Quite the opposite: it is about the life force, the instinct to survive, the drawn breath and first bleat of lamb or child. It is about a life saved, to the relief of a watching crowd. It's about my pride in my mother, the 'heroine'. There is a distinction between the 'voice' of the poet – the particular music and style by which we recognise a poet – and the voice of memory, recalled by the child inside me, the voice used to tell the remembered story. An example of such language is, 'my mother gave a stranger's child her breath'. This was my childish, uninformed description of mouth-to-mouth resuscitation. The choice of the word 'bleating', as the child drew her breath, turns the saved girl into a newborn lamb. The word comes from a lifetime of seeing lambs born, of watching a ewe drink the birth-fluids from its lamb the moment it is born. The birth-waters are exchanged for breath, water for air. The lamb is not a water baby, but born to breathe air, and to live, like the girl in the lake. The past, the forgotten and half-remembered, return whenever I visit Cold Knap, and say my own little nursery rhyme:

All lost things lie under closing water
in that lake with the poor man's daughter.

Postscript. In January, 2016, I received an email from a stranger, a retired teacher who had returned to Wales after a working life in England. She read the poem, and had long considered writing to me. Marion was the girl in the lake.

Cold Knap Lake

We once watched a crowd
pull a drowned child from the lake.
Blue lipped and dressed in water's long green silk
she lay for dead.

Then kneeling on the earth,
a heroine, her red head bowed,
her wartime cotton frock soaked,
my mother gave a stranger's child her breath.
The crowd stood silent,
drawn by the dread of it.

The child breathed, bleating
and rosy in my mother's hands.
My father took her home to a poor house
and watched her thrashed for almost drowning.

Was I there?
Or is that troubled surface something else
shadowy under the dipped fingers of willows
where satiny mud blooms in cloudiness
after the treading, heavy webs of swans
as their wings beat and whistle on the air?

All lost things lie under closing water
in that lake with the poor man's daughter.

JOURNAL

The Deep Sleep of Trees
January 2018

Twelfth Night. We take down the tree, the holly and the larch branches that annually deck the hall – some for the bonfire, some kindling for the stove, some for the compost heap. Into the box marked 'Christmas' go the angels, baubles, glitter, tree lights, the wrapping paper saved, smoothed and folded, all to be stowed for next year, and the year after that.

It is an annual moment of clearance and renewal. A brief sense of loss gives way to pleasure as the uncluttered architecture of the room is set free, its space and height, its oak frame – green oak from the Gwaun valley in Pembrokeshire – the south gable wall to my right, glazed all the way up to the apex, and, before me as I work at the table, the long, glazed east wall which frames the winter garden, and beyond it, through bare laburnum branches, a glimpse of fields rising above the Glowan valley; to my right, through the bare branches of the sleeping beech, the far blue profile of Llanllwni mountain. Sometimes the eastern view brings me a fiery sunrise, sometimes a huge red moon, rising until it looks in through the gable. This morning I am blinded by the dazzle of the low winter sun.

10 January

For the first time in forty years we are without animals. No dog, no cat, no sheep. Our Welsh collie, Siani, died aged fifteen. Her companion was our last cat, Siwan, who came to us out of nowhere as a kitten when Siani was a puppy. She sniffed Siani's body, and fled in terror. She ate nothing and was repeatedly sick for nine days. The vet examined her, found nothing physically wrong, and said, 'This is grief.' She never recovered from Siani's death. She was twenty-two when the vet gave that last injection. Animals are more than we know. Mysterious, wordless. We can't hope to fathom their instincts and emotions.

We buried her next to Siani below the far beech hedge. I recall a long-ago piece in the *Guardian* about burying pets in the garden, 'On the Last Day, when the bodies of the dead are resurrected, what an upheaval there will be on our lawn!' Remembering it made me smile, though we are sad, for the first time without a cat or dog.

Wild creatures are our consolation: the hare returns every day, and today a heron came to visit. We often see the heron standing still for hours at the edge of the pond in the field, a stick-thin cleric on 'the heron-priested shore'. One day recently, all elegance lost, a heron shuffled over the lawn and heaved itself onto the terrace, clumsy as an old bishop weighed down by voluminous robes. It saw us, took fright and hauled itself and its cassocky plumage onto the terrace wall, smashing a flowerpot as it went. Only when it lifted on the air, wings outspread in flight, legs and plumage folded neatly against its body, did the heron regain its slender grace.

*

In a recurring dream I am lost in a winter wood. It is safe, silent, hallowed, a lofty, sacred architecture. I am happy walking in the wood, along its aisles under a branchy roof lit as if by clerestories, glades opening like side chapels. I imagine, once upon a time, when the whole of Britain was clothed in forest how our ancestors, living under trees, must have dreamed the first cathedral, the first hymn to awe.

Waking from my tree-dream to a cold, dark day I think of how we and our earth are alive because of trees. It is more than physical, more than a question of shelter and shade and oxygen, or the provision of habitat for a million creatures. Trees nourish our imagination, and have always done so. Forests covered the earth before the first 'Adam', the first 'Eve' evolved, perhaps stepping out of the sea. Trees taught us shelter, art, architecture, ideas, wonder. Trees were the metaphors that made us dream: a child's den in a wood, a hollow tree, hut, house, hall, roof, architrave, aisle, arcade, clerestory – the luminous level over the triforium of a cathedral, where the light gets in. Trees live so long that they are history. I think of the Pontfadog oak, Britain's oldest tree until a storm brought it down in April 2013:

its hollow heart a cave for lovers,
cell for the holy, shelter for sheep, cover
for soldier, thief, fugitive, conspirator, older
than cathedrals, its branches caught the stars,
made cruck and cradle, roof-beams, rafters,
fuel for the hearth; pollarded, sprouted, spared
when Henry Plantagenet razed Ceiriog woods.

*

It has been a bitter winter. Politics, weather, a divided nation, hard words. The worst political crisis in my memory goes on and on. Long hours of darkness. Days of strife. Now every day yields a few more minutes of light as we creep towards the spring equinox. No bird sings but the robin, his solo sounding the sweeter in the great silence, so clear and strong today. His song holds ground, lifts the heart, brings hope. A wren darts over the terrace between the pots, finding shelter where it can. Every winter we notice maybe a dozen wrens cwtched into the old swallows' nest under the eaves outside the porch door. A cwtch of wrens: I offer it as a collective noun for sheltering wrens. When, coming home after dark, we open the outer door and turn on the light, in a blink we miss the shadow-dash of a bird from the eaves into the porch. Stepping through the inner door into the kitchen we miss the second flight too, the bird is too small, too quick. The extension built onto our old house is a single open space from the kitchen into the glazed, oak-framed living room, and for the twelve days of Christmas I swear there is always a wren on its favourite perch above the angel's head at the top of our tree, glittering and multiplied in the glass against the black night. We find the wren in the morning, and release it into the garden. It will be back!

January 2019

Twelfth Night, another year over and Christmas done, we take down the tree, the holly and the ivy, and the fret of larch twigs on the roof-trusses above our heads, where a gold-robed plaster angel flew for twelve days. We pack the baubles and glitter into their box to be stored in the loft for another year.

Swept of clutter, the room looks young again, expecting light, a stir of spring. A pair of jays comes to the feeder. They wait a moment in the old plum tree until it looks safe from magpies. Two lesser spotted woodpeckers are here every day. Usually a good sleeper, in these restless times I wake from a vivid dream several times a night, my head full of words, flocks and paragraphs, rhythms and rhymes and images, as well as ridiculous rubbish like times tables, anagrams, argument, a passing whirr of words as a grey winter morning begins. It is telling me that I need to get on with writing. But where will my word-flocks settle?

*

A new year, a new project. The Woodland Grant has come. Six and a half acres on our two steepest slopes, the *fronnau*,[1] will be converted from grazing land into woodland. Our dream of trees is coming true. In the autumn of 2018, the nesting season over, fledgelings safely flown, contractors, organised by our ecology advisor, Alison, cleared wide aisles in the gorse to prepare the slopes for planting in March this year.

I settle to write these pages over ten years since I wrote 'At the Source', plundering my journals and memory. Much has changed and is changing at Blaen Cwrt, on the land and about the house. The old longhouse looks much as it must have done two hundred years ago, graciously accepting the thirty-foot oak-and-glass space David designed for the south end. This morning it is flooded with sunlight, as the old house with its two tiny windows could never be. We still 'warm our hands with apple wood', though it is more likely to be ash, chestnut, sycamore these days, as old trees sickened and had to be felled. Nothing is wasted. All is dried to be used for carpentry, mulch or warmth. Newly felled is an old grove of larch which showed signs of suffering a newly diagnosed disease. Clearing the larch grove is part of the twelve-year woodland plan.

---

1 slopes.

The way we work our eighteen acres is evolving, as grazing pasture becomes woodland. All our sloping land, six and a half acres, will become a continuous plantation of trees extending from Fron[1] Blaen Cwrt across Fron Felen[2] to our farthest border at the end of the old oak wood. Only the level land at the tops of the fields, running above the new woods and the ancient oak wood, will be kept for occasional grazing by some of our neighbour Gethin's sheep. It's our small contribution to reforesting the earth.

Fifty years ago, when I first saw Blaen Cwrt, it was a derelict longhouse, 'two rooms, waking and sleeping'. The little *parlwr*[3] where Marged slept, after the deaths of her aunt and grandfather, is now our bathroom, the open mouth of her tiny grate, under the huge north chimney, a nook for bathroom things, the chimney above blocked to keep out the wind, the birds and the bees. The next 'room' under the single long roof – now our bedroom – was once the old *scubor*.[4] When we first came here, summer-camping in the ruin, the barn was home to a tawny owl and its haunting psalm. Its Welsh name, *gwdihŵ*, imitates the sound of its cry. Sometimes, at night, we hear it still.

The last space at the north end, the old *beudy*[5] built against the end of the longhouse, became the study where, floor to eaves, books insulate the rear wall, the gable wall and the corner once filled by the manger. The old wide doorway, once open to the cobbled yard, is now closed by three casement windows above a window seat. Two centuries ago, when the house was raised from the stones of the fields, Blaen Cwrt's

---

1 slope.

2 the golden slope.

3 parlour.

4 barn.

5 cowshed.

blank rear wall was built into the bank, its two small east-facing windows letting in a squint of light. Shelter, not light, was the priority of the rural poor.

Letting the light in, opening the spaces, we have combined preservation with improvement. Blaen Cwrt is a rare surviving, un-bungalowed example of the classic, single-storey stone Cardiganshire longhouse, typically two rooms and a barn under a single long roof. A central door between a pair of small windows, the house-roof flanked by two huge chimneys, make a pleasing symmetry. Blaen Cwrt's dairy was built on the south end, the *beudy* on the north. It once overlooked a yard, a vegetable patch, a few plum trees, a sour old apple tree, a pigsty, a scratching ground for hens. We identified the remains of the old piggery, the *cwt mochyn,* from pigs' jaws among the fallen stones of the sty. The dairy is now our tiny kitchen – a *gegin fach*[6] – which steps through the partly removed external dairy wall into the generous space of a new *gegin fawr,*[7] open to this oak-framed, glass-walled room where I write. To east and south are glass doors to the stone terrace, laid where the farmyard used to be. The new leaves the old untouched, but neighboured.

This is where, after the deaths in the 1930s of her grandfather and her aunt, Marged, middle-aged, defeated by poverty and loneliness, died. Neighbours heard her cow lowing to be milked, and found Marged's body in the barn. She had hanged herself.

My husband's Mamgu[8] spent a few years as a young girl living with relatives in the nearby village, and Marged was her friend. Before Mamgu's death at the age of a hundred and one, David brought her to see Blaen Cwrt. She showed

---

6 small kitchen, or scullery.

7 big kitchen.

8 grandmother.

us how the two rooms were used in the old days, where Marged and her aunt slept in the loft, her grandfather in a cupboard bed against the back wall of their kitchen, now our sitting room.

Old maps show a track passing the gate, where the tarmac lane now runs down to the valley. The 'source' of the Llymru,[1] south of the glazed gable, is the well from which she drew her water. The stream swells to run south along the bank, becomes the Bwdram, and flows downhill to join the river Glowan in the valley. The word *llymru* was brought into English by Shakespeare as 'flummery', lace at the wrists and throats of courtiers.

From the early 1970s, Blaen Cwrt was our summer house. In 1985, my first January alone at Blaen Cwrt, it snowed. Roads were blocked. David, still working and living in Aberystwyth, joined me at weekends. I had good neighbours, and tractors kept the roads clear, but I was snow-surrounded. Arthur Scargill led the miners' strike. I had no wood, and the last coal I ever burned was German. I often thought about Marged. For me, camping in Blaen Cwrt was an adventure, but for her, in the early twentieth century, it was poverty, loneliness, hunger, cold. For the rural poor, January was a bitter month.

*

The white winters of 1942 and 1947 were legendary. How many Januaries do I remember? Every wet, grey January retreats into the fog, but the snowy ones of childhood are luminous ice-globes. I shake one, and see my mother draw back blue and white bedroom curtains to show me a snow-world through the bars of my cot, the white garden, the park, the frozen lake.

---

1 the foam on milk or beer.

The January my sister was born, 1942, my beautiful red-haired mother sat pale and tired in her blue velvet dressing gown downstairs in our house in Lakeside, Barry, in a room they called the 'lounge'. My new sister slept swaddled in a carrycot. Spreadeagled on the floor was the polar bear skin my father bought in a house sale, and on its coarse white fur lay my small pile of Christmas presents – home-made, or second-hand, rustling, wrapped and beribboned treasures. The room was warmed by a two-bar electric fire with a bed of glowing embers pretending to be coal. Beyond the bay window where, for twelve magic days, the Christmas tree trembled with tinsel glitter, were the park and the frozen lake, a white world where a polar bear might wander with a child on its back.

The winter of 1941–42 was one of the coldest of the twentieth century. It was the first white winter which memory and research recall. The temperature was well below freezing point from the beginning of January until the end of March. I was four years old. Every day after lunch from when I was two, I was put down on the bearskin for an afternoon nap. I would nap nowhere else. I rode the Arctic wastes and frozen seas of Barry on his scratchy pelt. I lay close to his head and fed him with pieces of rusk, which my mother later had to 'hoover' from his wide-open jaws.

I loved the bear. He came from a big house, and before that from the Arctic, a frozen country at the top of the world, which my father showed me on the globe he bought me. My bear was alive. I rode him across the snowy road and the frozen lake. My hour on the bearskin gave my mother 'peace and quiet' to have a lie-down in her room, 'cold cream' on her face, her red curls in a hairnet. I had hours to pretend, to read, draw, to play alone between waking and a bedtime story, not fussed over, taught or tested.

A few years ago, locked in memory's lair all the years of my life, the bear woke in my adult poet's head, plodded silently through the snow, and at last insisted on my protection. Tutoring a poetry course, I set a group of writers the task of remembering an object from childhood, of setting the remembered scene and seeing where it would lead them. Use memory, your five senses, and the sixth sense, your imagination, I said. While they wrote I thought of my bear. I wrote 'Polar' at the silent table. A first verse remembered the scene:

> Snowlight and sunlight, the lake glacial.
> Too bright to open my eyes
> in the dazzle and doze
> of a distant January afternoon.

The years of the white bear – 1942, and 1947, and others when snow fell deep and crisp and even out-glow every grey January. Garden, road, park, were all luminous in a transfiguration that made my heart hot, my skin prick, and my feet jump with restlessness to go out to play in the snow-world of stories.

I ran out of the back door into six inches of lying snow, to be shocked by the cold. The plushy sound of it underfoot, the cold on my face, were new sensations. My mother wrapped me as well as she could in my fawn coat with its brown velvet collar, hand-knitted scarf and mittens, wellington boots stuffed with socks. No tights, no trousers, just a short tartan skirt above soon-to-be-frozen legs, chapped knees and chilblained toes. Later I walked on the ice – on Cold Knap lake! – and was towed by Daddy in a home-made sledge. A first flake on winter air still brings me that electric charge.

Dead birds lay on the snow, corpses in a war. War! Birds starved to death for lack of bread, as every crumb and crust was saved for the table. Bread, eggs, sugar, fruit, meat, were scarce, or rationed. I had never seen a banana, an orange, a melon, except in picture books. Once, a Belgian ship's captain, a friend of my father, gave me a mango. They had known each other in my father's former merchant navy days, when he worked as a ship's wireless officer – the ship's 'Sparks' – receiving and sending morse-coded messages in a circle as wide as long wave would reach across the ocean. On the day of the mango, the captain's ship had docked in Barry, or Cardiff, and my father took me and my mother to meet him. I was about two or three years old. The mango was green and red, heavy to hold, and the juice ran down my chin and fingers onto my coat.

In times of rationing, it was against the law to bring eggs home from the family's farm in Pembrokeshire, though my father regularly did so, sharing them with neighbours, friends and colleagues. As engineer-in-charge, Outside Broadcasts, BBC Wales (I quote from inside the cover of my treasured copy of his small Welsh-English dictionary), his was a reserved occupation, so he was not called up to the war. Instead, he travelled the length and breadth of Wales for his work, and brought home to the family whatever food he came across, home-churned butter, eggs, a flitch of bacon, gifts from farms where he was known and welcomed.

We children foraged too – windfalls from other people's gardens where branches leaned over pavements; hedge fruits, wild plums, blackberries, and, once, the greatest treasure trove of all: crates of oranges spilt on the beach of the Little Harbour in Barry. I had only seen an orange in storybooks. These were real. They came from *The Jamaica Planter*, a ship struck by a mine in Barry harbour, scattering its cargo of oranges on the oily sand beside their burst crates. I filled my skirt and home-made knickers-to-match, (elasticated, baggy, and useful for storage) and carried them bumpily home. My mother scrubbed them clean, and made something of them. They were disappointingly sour. I preferred the concentrated government orange juice then allocated to children.

*

January 2019

The last two weeks of Poetry Live. Birmingham, Nottingham, Reading and Bath, on to Cardiff and thence home for the weekend. Then on the train again, through the snow to Leeds where, alarmed by the weather, schools cancelled, and we lost some of our student audience. Thence over the snowbound flatlands of eastern England to Cambridge, and on to London, and Manchester, journeying through a lonely, bleak, grey winter world, across a wasteland heavy with political foreboding, a black tunnel under the earth. My spirits begin to lift on the homebound stretch from the Welsh-English border to the Irish Sea, as the train travels between the snow-covered mountains from Shrewsbury to Aberystwyth. Snow, snowlight and the prospect of home, our garden and fields transfigured by unblemished snow. Why do those dark train journeys across strangers' country trouble me so deeply?

*

The gorse has been cleared. Soon the contractors will be here to fence the slopes, to separate our future woodland from fields where a small flock of our neighbour's sheep comes to graze between times. Winter. In the time of the deep sleep of trees, our dream of woods begins.

January 2020

A new page. The hunt is out. With or without a living prey to rip to bits, they are not allowed on our land, so David set off for a walk over the fields to show them we are watching.

He'd been spending hours and energy hacking at the ash root. It is still taller than he is, the size of a small garden shed, and no doubt there is still a mass of ash tree-root as deep and as wide under the earth. He must reduce it to make room for scaffolding to stand firm, as he works on cladding the west wall of the studio.

Dylan left after lunch to visit Peter in Cardiff, before returning to Southampton tomorrow. We will miss him.

3 January

A beautiful day, silent, still, sunlight on the far fields. A four-year Boris Johnson-led Tory government begins with threats of a no-deal Brexit, and further sorrows: NHS deals with Trump's America, budget cuts to all the things we hold important, and the prospect of world disorder under two incompetent yellow-haired men.

There is an ominous rumour in the air, a bat-disease in China contagious to humans. We need the consoling beauty of trees, and this ice-cold golden weather.

The Highest Wind in the World
February 2018

3 February

We woke to ice-cold sunlight. I can hardly read a word on the screen or page for the dazzling stare of the low sun. 'Look at us,' say the trees, the fields and the sky, 'not the damn screen!'

Beyond the glass walls snow swirls out of a darkening sky, white feathers settling on the terrace, the lawn, the fields. Then just as suddenly the sky clears to blue. Sunlight on the lawn, the far fields lit. It is holy, a transfiguration. Snow always sets my heart racing, as every snowy day of my life returns to turn winter into the land of the Snow Queen.

I stand a moment to relish the vista we have made down the path through the gap in the laburnum bank to the far end of the garden. It runs past a clipped mixed hedge on the right, planted years ago to separate the garden from the fields, in particular from the home field, Cae Blaen Cwrt. To the left of the path, raised vegetable beds and the russet wall of clipped beech mark the edge, and show the way.

Perspective. A view narrowing down a walk to tempt foot and eye. At the end of the path is a Japanese maple, a red acer, leafless now in the scribble of bare winter trees, but beside it a small white table and two garden chairs mark the spot. They are placed to measure the distance from here to there, to suggest a place to pause, gaze, and listen. In the garden of a grand house a statue would gratify the desire for a punctuation mark at the end of a vista. In our garden two plastic chairs and a table do the job, and are more inviting, suggesting a mug of tea after garden work, and in summer a sip of wine after a day on our computers. From April to October a flaming tree marks the spot, an acer, Persian-carpet red in summer, auburn in autumn. There are not enough words for that red.

Today, lying snow miles north-east on the Cambrian mountains of mid-Wales, our trees bare and the air clear, we have had a revelation, a piece of far away, snow-lit topography. A distant and usually obscure feature as we look through binoculars straight down the garden to the eastern horizon, we have seen it before, wondered a moment and put it out of mind. The coincidence of snow on a distant mountain peak – only the summits are snow-covered – winter sunlight, leafless trees, and an operated knee giving me time to stand and stare, offers a vision, geographical, mythical, which for forty winters we have been too busy to understand and name. A snow-lit summit, glimpsed and wondered about when trees are bare, the air ice-clear, and light illuminates a distant mountain.

In imagination, this February day, I cross the terrace and follow the grass path to where our garden ends and a neighbour's land descends into the Glowan valley, to rise a crow-flying mile away, where the hamlet of Pisgah is marked by a red barn. On a rare day like this, through binoculars, just to the right of the red barn, we can see the pale shoulder. It is just a glimpse, but the light is perfect. We get out the map and compass to confirm our suspicion: it is the summit of Pumlumon, many miles north-east; a shining crown, birthplace of Sabrina, source of the Severn, the Wye, the Rheidol. There, two of Arthur's knights, Cai and Bedwyr, sought to pluck a bristle of the wild boar in their list of the feats that must be achieved before the giant could be slain and his daughter Olwen set free to marry Culhwch.

> 'As Cai and Bedwyr sat on a beacon carn on the summit of Pumlimmon, in the highest wind that ever was in the world, they looked around them, and saw a great smoke towards the south, afar off, which did not bend in the wind'.
> (*The Mabinogi*)

So the peak of Pumlumon is visible from here, where I write. The thought brings close the near and the far, the present and the past, the facts and the myth. I relish the fabulous connection, the myth and the geography. The sight line runs from where I stand in this room, across the terrace, the lawn, through the gap in the wild laburnum bank and on to the end of the garden. On the same grass path I often see wild creatures: in spring a fox quick as flame seen off by nesting magpies; often, a hare. Just one more step and I leap giant leagues to a mountain peak and its mythical past. It is poetry's touchpaper.

Had we been completely well, busy, at work, we might not have made time to find and name the snowy peak. Had David still been working full-time in Aberystwyth, instead of at home, self-employed again, we might have let the thought pass, half-wondering what it was. Kept in by the weather, coughs and colds, we had time to gaze at the view, to stare into distance, into history, mythology, to wonder at far horizons and old stories.

*

The way we live is changing. Two years ago, we handed over our little flock of sheep and the use of our five fields to our young neighbour, Gethin. No longer need we go out with a torch last thing at night and again at dawn to check the ewes. It is good to see ewes in the fields, but as lambing time draws close, Gethin takes them home to his family's farm, a few miles away. I miss being on watch when new lambs arrive. I miss the touch, the weight and smell of them, their small, bubbling cries.

It is hard to get used to being free of all animals, but for our visiting hare. Free to come home late, to rise late, to enjoy slow Sunday mornings, to travel, to work, to accept invitations to gigs. We work because we must, and because we love it. Where did eight decades go? I don't *feel* different. At the first flake of snow I am that child again.

*

On a cold, dark February day, our ecologist, Alison, brings us news – the application for a woodland planting grant she submitted on our behalf to the Welsh Government and the Woodland Trust, has been accepted.

Together we spread the map of our eighteen acres of land on the table, and mark out the area planned for woodland. Alison is as pleased as we are. A dream of trees: sapling woods planted over six and a half acres. She marks the four-metre-wide aisles to be cleared in the gorse-banks for tree planting, leaving bands of gorse for nesting birds. A twelve-year plan, preparation to begin in the autumn when the birds have flown the nests, and gorse can safely be cleared to make the ground ready for the saplings. At once I feel a surge of purpose, energy and optimism, just thinking about 'our' new trees. They are the future. At last I am cured of missing our sheep, of our duties caring for them, of the joy of finding a newborn lamb in the corner of Cae Blaen Cwrt in the early morning, since Gethin took over the use of our grazing land and the care of our small flock of Speckled Faced ewes. His sheep have white faces, and over a few seasons the characteristic black-speckled faces of our flock have disappeared as the genes of his sheep prevail. I miss their speckled faces. It is strange to have no shepherding to do.

I am not drawn to the word 'sensible'. In my mind's thesaurus, 'retirement' is a grey word which drains me of energy. It leaves my imagination bereft. No sheep, no animals, no changing seasons on our own land, even, as suggested by one helpful friend, moving from Blaen Cwrt to live in town instead of here at nine hundred feet. No excitement at falling snow, no prospect of being snowed in, no thinking, 'I'd better make bread in case we can't get out.'

Woodland is Blaen Cwrt's new future. My future is to write about it. All our steep land will be fenced off, grazing confined to the level strip of high land that runs to our farthest border. Trees will cover the slopes, Fron Blaen Cwrt[1] and Fron Felen,[2] the former slope named after our house, the latter for the golden gorse that gives it its colour. A twelve-year plan, scrub clearance at the end of summer, fencing and ground-preparation in winter, tree planting in spring. Twelve years to watch trees grow.

19 February

Arriving home from Cardiff on Sunday night after the Cornerstone Poetry Festival, we discovered we had a visitor. David opened the porch door and the kitchen door, switched on the lights, and a great tit flew into the house. After much kerfuffle and shooing, waving our arms, switching off lights and opening doors and roof windows (letting out all the heat) we persuaded it out of the dark kitchen into the lit porch, and thence into the dark garden. Over the next hours, as we ate our supper and sipped a glass of wine, it tapped on the kitchen window. Then we turned out the kitchen lights and repaired to the sitting room and the wood-burning stove. The great tit, attracted by the light, appeared at the small gable window high in the wall beside the chimney breast, where it resumed its tap-tapping to be let in. We can't call this house our own.

---

1 slope.

2 the golden slope.

Wrens, frogs, newts, a robin, mice, sometimes a toad, think that we are the visitors, and that it is they who really live here.

February 2019

An exciting morning. The contractors are here to prepare the land for the new woodland. Local men, Tomi and his son John, have come to fence the slopes to mark grazing land from areas proposed for woodland. The saplings must be planted in the next few weeks. Our dream of trees is taking root.

I am stirred by the idea of a tree book. I have mulled for days, weeks, but could not see the scaffolding which a new book of prose could use to build itself, one word upon another, sentence on sentence, the shape of a chapter. I could not hear the first phrase. My mind is full of trees, birds and words. Somehow root and word must work together. Now that the land is fenced neat as stanzas on a page, and ready for planting, I begin to see and to hear lines, the whisper of wind in sapling trees, words and woods rooting, sounding space, reaching deeper, higher, wider, season after season. I see a green future, watching our trees grow, remembering trees that made me: tree-dens in Porthkerry woods, Barry, elm trees in the grounds of my school, the silver birch outside my bedroom window in Penarth – they were my first architecture. To listen. To let words speak.

The words come flocking, as wild birds will when the seasons change. Years ago, when we bought our land, we gradually replaced all the hedges which had been grubbed out by a butcher from Buckinghamshire who came for a few years, went bankrupt and left. As the trees and hedges grew – hazel, rowan, wild cherry, blackthorn, hawthorn – and the bleak emptiness leafed, blossomed, filled the space, for the first time we heard the song-thrush at Blaen Cwrt. Some years ago, below our old oak wood, we had a grove of oak saplings planted – a gift from one of David's clients who had no space for them. The old wood, a hectare of sessile oaks on a south-facing slope, floods with bluebells from late April to early May, and now the young trees too stand in blue every spring. It was to protect the old bluebell wood that we bought the eighteen acres of land in the first place.

I await a first sentence, recite the list of species to be planted in our dreamed wood. Their very names bring the itch of words to my fingertips: oak, hazel, rowan, wild cherry, birch. Something is beginning. A bud. A leaf. The downward tickle of a root.

*

The fencing is done, neatly marking the old track that runs through the gorse, with just one gate so we can drive the track but keep the sheep away from the new woodland. Above the track, the gorse slopes rise steeply, and below it the newly fenced land slopes down to the road. Planting time comes for the saplings, delivered to the house in bags. They lie waiting their moment outside the barn. We recite the labels: Sessile Oak, Downy Birch, Hazel, Rowan, Wild Cherry. The land is ready. The team begins work next week.

*

Between August 2018 and January 2019, when nests had emptied and fledgelings flown, aisles were cleared of gorse and scrub, strips between the aisles left uncut for next year's nesting birds. The high land that runs above the slopes to the far end of the old oak wood will be kept for occasional grazing, fenced off from the six and a half acres proposed for the new woodland. Four thousand, three hundred saplings. Twenty years after buying our eighteen acres, it is thrilling to let woods spread across the slopes from end to end. Including the old wood, half our land will be covered by trees.

*

From where I work I look left into the kitchen and on through the open door into the sitting room, where the view ends with a lamp in the corner which, at night, lights a wall of books. Ahead of me is the view north-east, across the terrace, the lawn, down the path to the far border and the highest wind in the world. To my right, beech trees, and between the tree trunks a glimpse of faraway Llanllwni mountain. There is pleasure in perspective, indoors and out, long views through a house or a garden, glimpses of half-hidden rooms and spaces, as in paintings by Vermeer.

*

Planting a tree is a ceremony, the start of something. We plant a tree to remember a birth, a death. The oak we planted for David's father is now a great tree. Glyndŵr's Oak. I look over the Middle Lawn to where Glyn's oak stands at the edge of the field. The red maple we planted for my mother stands in the rain, every bud held in a raindrop-globe. Each bud will open into a three-lobed leaf, Persian red turning to flame before it falls. It remembers her beautiful red hair, and the way she loved feeling leaf-silk between her fingers as she walked in a garden.

At the far end of our garden, under the giant leap across geography and myth to the summit of Pumlumon, is the acer that marks the end of the path. I call it 'Euros's tree', after the neighbour who planted it for me. A prospect needs a punctuation mark. From here to the sitting room, the lamp does it. A garden vista of a grand house might conclude with a statue. Before Euros planted our acer, he stood a few hundred yards away at the far end of the path holding the tree and a spade, signalling, while I stood by the glass wall in this room, signalling back: Left a bit! Back a bit! Thumbs up! Perfect! He dug the hole, placed the tree, replaced the earth around it and trod it down. It has flourished, grown taller, wider, a flame of a tree for eight months of the year.

Some time later, we heard that he had died. 'Euros's tree' remembers him, and so do we, as we look down that path.

We plant a tree knowing that it will outlive us. Perhaps as we do so, we half-hope the tree will contain us, holding our soul in its sap, root and foliage, and live for centuries, growing on as part of us who walk the land, use it, look after it and love it. And maybe, once we are gone, its roots 'remember' the tread of our feet on the ground.

Because we humans lived for, probably, thousands of years in forests, trees are rooted in our imagination, language and understanding of the earth. Woods and forests have taught us how to live. From great trees our ancestors learned loftiness and scale, how to dream, how to raise great buildings, how to worship and how to live. A forest canopy is reimagined as a cathedral with its pillars, aisles and clerestories. I remember when, as a child, a friend and I built ourselves a house. It was a den in a hollow oak in Porthkerry woods, Barry. I can still feel the sound waves of a train crossing the viaduct nearby, and the tide breaking on the pebbles of the beach, vibrating in the 'walls' of that first 'house'.

Last week of February 2019

Just three weeks since days and nights of bitter cold, February forgets itself and sails into its last days in a heatwave. Heatwave! *Ton wres*! Ceredigion in February breaks the British record for the time of year at well over twenty degrees Celsius. Three weeks after snow it is warm as summer, warm enough for lunch on the terrace. There is a bumblebee in the pieris. A butterfly on the wing slows and settles on a bare beech twig against the light of the sun. The new hedge of hazels on the bank along the lane behind the house, planted just a few weeks ago, is stirring into life – buds swell, a leaf unfolds. Everywhere buds are ready to open, 'like something almost being said'.[1]

This unseasonal weather makes me uneasy. I am anxious for the spring foliage, for the pulse of new growth setting buds on the move too soon. The days grow longer, but night frosts can bite as late as May and ice-winds roar in from the north.

Noon. Lunch at the garden table. It is beautiful, but worrying. This is summer heat. This time last year we had snow, and there were gritter-lorries on the roads. I worry that the heat will confuse the birds and insects, deceive the trees, stir the sap, loosen buds, set things on the move too early. Even here, at nine hundred feet, we are experiencing the highest February temperatures ever recorded. I would be happier to wait for a real and timely spring, an April of opening buds, the beech trees' first, delicious green moment outside the glass walls of this room, when the south gable will fill with long, dipping boughs of 'beechen green'.

David comes in to cool down after barrowing stony soil from behind the house. In through the wide-open doors come the flies, hatched, woken, hungry. I must welcome them. News is ominous: Earth is losing its insects, essential to life,

---

1 Philip Larkin.

to pollination, plants, food for humans or animals. I think I already knew this. I recall standing at a lectern in a theatre reading to an audience, trying to avoid crushing a creature the size of a full stop crawling the open page of the book from which I was reading. Then there are the nameless ones about the house. The glass doors are open to a warm, spring-like day, and in come the flies, hatched, woken by the warmth. I am half-glad to see them. If the earth loses its insects, without them we all die. So come in, flies! Settle, as every spring, on the warmed glass inside the roof-windows. Welcome the crane fly on the kitchen window, rescue the spider from the bath, let live the creature on the worktop.

Dusk at the end of a beautiful day. Rose light fades on bare branches, the stems of young trees, last year's dead flower heads, brown stalks from last summer. It is warm enough to have a dusk drink on the terrace. This is not natural. Our pleasure is shadowed by unease.

February 2020

Something alarming is happening in China. A virus, caught, they say, from bushmeat sold in Chinese live-meat markets, has spread to human victims in Wuhan. It is a disease of bats, and there, on the news, we see live bats hanging in rows over market stalls, and people moving among them. It has passed from animal to human, and is moving fast, across borders, boundaries, seas. A new plague.

The Silence

A primitive life form out of the air,
a seed in the gut of a hen, neck wrung,
still warm from a market stall,
where bushmeat is sold dead and alive
with fish, beast and fowl.

Rabies, Ebola, Marburg, Hendra, Nipah, SARS, MERS.
Pretty names on the wing, in the gut, in the blood of a bat,
the winged mammal Leonardo caught and cut,
probing its body for its engineered parts,
the spread webs of its wings for the secret of flight.

Isolate. Isola. Island. Ynys. We are alone,
alone with the page, the screen, our view south
clear to Llanllwni mountain over the brow of a field,
and sometimes, to the east, that distant peak,
the dreamed summit of Pumlumon.

There's a collared dove on the grass,
rose-beige bird with its necklace of jet.
Hope comes with its mate, with summer,
the world in remission this darkening hour
before dusk, as birds self-isolate to the trees.

Birds. Words on a wire, on radio waves in the air,
the transmission of fear through a darkening sky
as numbers rise of the sick and the dead.
Doors are closing, festivals folding their tents.
Music is silenced.

The lights are going out.
The curtain falls on a darkened stage.

To the Woods
March 2018

Coughs, colds, days of lethargy stole February and part of March. And it snowed. It was bitterly cold and the house was difficult. Every room was in disarray, the beautiful new bookshelves David is making unfinished; piles of books wait to be taken to the second-hand bookshop in Aberystwyth; a sideboard, displaced by the new bookshelves, fills the hall, and there is furniture to sell, garments for the clothes bank, stuff waiting to be driven to the dump. The temperature in our bedroom dropped to freezing point. We were saved by our electric blanket, and a duck-down duvet deep as the kind of summer cloud which floated over the hills and far away in the Ernest H. Shepard illustrations of A.A. Milne.

It was certainly cold here, but being close to the Irish Sea and the relative warmth of the Atlantic, we in Ceredigion experienced just enough snow for a miraculous transfiguration: the land luminous, the terrace, garden, fields and slopes rising on the other side of the Glowan valley became a shining new world. Then there was that mythological vision, the glimpse of the distant, usually invisible peak of Pumlumon.

Weather forecasters called the snow that fell on England, Scotland, and the extreme east of Wales the 'Beast from the East'. The ice-winds came from the east and the north-east, and West Wales was sheltered from the worst of the blizzards by the Cambrian mountains. It snowed enough here to be beautiful, the garden and the shining land beyond our glass walls enchanting. But it was cold. I have never felt so cold. I am never ill, rarely tired, rarely feel the cold. All new experience is useful, however painful. David recovered, then so did I, but I could not settle to write. A first word! That was all I asked!

March 2019

Hallelujah! Our trees have been planted! Four thousand, three hundred saplings stand in their guards, such a crowd crossing our slopes bearing their buds like shawled babies, as refugees moved from the place of their cultivation to where they are welcome to make their home, to grow into great trees, seed themselves and become a forest that lives forever. The sapling woods now cover all the sloping ground that runs from Cae Bach to the farthest border of our land, and down to the road. It is thrilling to see them.

*

I am learning about trees. A mature tree drinks one hundred gallons of water drawn from the deep ground, and exhales it into the air. It provides oxygen for four people to breathe. Once our infant woods are grown, 4,000 trees will give oxygen to 16,000 people. A small town. There will, one day, be woodland shade, shelter, paths, glades and avenues. They are living architecture. A wood or a forest is pillared and roofed with branches, foliage, light, shadows, alive with flocks and families of birds, birdsong, and, here in the west, the breath of the Atlantic in their leaves. They can feel the earth on the move, words on the wing.

Our young woodland, planted, and underplanted with woody shrubs, gives me a litany of names to recite like a rosary: Sessile Oak, Downy Birch, Rowan, Hazel, Wild Cherry. Now all they need is sun and rain to root, to bud, to leaf, to make shade and to hold the ground beneath, to reach down, to 'talk' to each other under the earth in the conversation of trees, the interaction of roots in a community in the deep soil, to grow tall and cast 'shadows numberless', to extend their branches for nesting birds and a million,

million insects. A tree's underground root system is as big as the crown in the sky.

For the time being I am content to be patient, and to observe them, in case I might catch the stir of a bud, the unfurling of a leaf. Watching a sapling grow teaches me the definition of slow. Yet it seemed no time at all that the hedges we had planted around our fields leafed, blossomed and fruited in just a few years, and our millennium hornbeam avenue is now a tunnel of green, the trees almost touching overhead.

I have a poem on my mind by the late, great Australian poet, Les Murray. He stayed here with us once after reading in Aberystwyth, a man great in thought, in girth, in nature, in spirituality, steeped in spiritual, rural and agricultural matters. In the poem titled, 'The Meaning of Existence', he wrote these words:

> Everything except language
> Knows the meaning of existence.
> Trees, planets, rivers, time
> Know nothing else.

Trees, planets, rivers, time know the meaning of existence. Living with trees, in hill country, at an altitude of nine hundred feet, where night skies are unpolluted by urban street lights, where we often see the planets, where a stream that rises from a mud-puddle in our garden joins the river Glowan at the bottom of the valley, and runs onwards to the river Teifi and the sea, where we are all too aware of the seasons, of time and the speed of its passing, I respond to the truth of these lines. My words and I know nothing. I reflect on Les's poem. Our beech, birch, chestnut, sycamore, ash, oak, willow, laburnum trees know the meaning of existence, because trees know nothing else. I had better be listening!

*

We see woods as we travel, and I think, 'trees'. But these days I am more considered. I want to identify trees, to name them, especially those trees which will form our new woodland, listing, one by one, each of the tree species to be planted on our land.

*

At the farthest end of our land an ancient wood of sessile oaks grows on a south-facing slope. At two and a half acres, it is a beautiful wood at all seasons, but for three weeks at the end of May the trees stand in a flood of bluebells. The sessile oak may have been among the first trees to colonise the tundra when the ice retreated at the end of the last Ice Age. It is the main species in our new woodland, where one thousand, three hundred will be planted: *Quercus petraea,* the mountain oak, a deciduous broadleaf tree native to Britain and Europe. Like the 'English', or pedunculate oak, it supports more wildlife than any other native tree.

We already know how well sessile oaks flourish here, and how they are home and shelter to many wild creatures. We see the accumulating excavation and building works of badgers at the wood's far end. We often see foxes there too. I once watched two foxes trot across my path close behind two men who were standing on the hedge bank, looking through binoculars across the fields. They were hunt followers baying for blood. The hunt is not allowed on our land, and, as I stood watching, their prey moved silently, safely over the grass behind their backs. The second fox paused, and looked at me with its characteristic fox-grin before it slipped into our wood. I held my breath, in complicit silence.

Overhead, in the oak wood's treetops, are nests of kites, crows and buzzards, and spotted woodpeckers live in hollow trunks. One summer twilight years ago, David and I sat in silence for hours at the edge of the wood, watching for badgers as dusk darkened to night. We saw no badgers, and when at last we gave up and rose to our feet, the wood erupted in a great agitation of wings. While we were sitting silently, the birds had flown home to their roosts one by one as quiet as ghosts; as we stood to leave, they all woke at once and rose into the air in a panic of wings and a rush of sound.

One of my favourite Welsh poets is Waldo Williams. For some years, as head teacher of Dinas Cross Village School, Waldo lived close to my grandmother's farm, and my father knew him. Once, six years old and walking the farm track with my father, I was introduced to a man walking towards us: 'Mr Williams, the poet'. He shook my hand. A moment long-forgotten, to be remembered decades later, its significance at last understood. It was a revelation. Propped against a wall on a shelf in this room, where I write at the dining table, is a small oak block into which an artist has carved a line from one of Waldo's poems:

> *Beth yw gweithio ond gwnaed cân o'r coed a'r gwenith?*
> (What is work but making a song of the wood and the wheat?)

Art and poetry. The wood and the wheat. The natural source of so much that we use and touch, live with, create with. Tools, materials, the breadboard which David made, and the loaf we slice on it, the paper on which these words will be printed, the books I read, the dining table where I write, remade for us by a carpenter out of an old hotel refectory table, the traditional library stick chair in which I sit to type these words, made for me in elm, ash and oak, with wedges of ebony, by John Brown of Pembrokeshire, maker of Welsh Stick Chairs. He only agreed to make me a chair if I sent him a poem. When the chair was ready, we drove to Fishguard to collect it. I remember him with a sonnet:

John, before the making of my chair
you asked me for a poem. As I choose now
your chair to make my little thing of air,
the perfect pen and page, so twenty years ago,
you chose wedge and dowel, the right piece of ash
to form the lovely curve where now I lean
to think a moment, wanting the words fresh.
My fingers tell the silk-slick ebony beads
where the sticks pierce the arm, the seat of elm.
Our songs are worked from the wood and the wheat.
Your work or mine, when art is at the helm
there's vertigo as mind and matter meet.
We leave our wake on water, in the grain of things,
with chisel or pen. Sometimes it sings.

Cerdd is Welsh for 'song', or 'poem'. Songs of the wood and the wheat. Where would we be without the poetry of such things?

The downy birch is one of the species planned for our new wood. One of the first trees I loved, almost as a friend, was a silver birch. I was ten years old. The birch was tall enough to reach the window of my attic bedroom on the third floor of our house in a town by the sea in Penarth, South Wales. On wild windy nights its fingers strummed the glass. On still summer days it was a whispering silver-green waterfall. Coleridge, seeing a birch beside the waters of a brook scattering over a rock, links the sounds, the 'silver' of the 'pendulous' foliage, with the falling waters.

Beneath yon birch with silver bark
And boughs so pendulous and fair,
The brook falls scattered down the rock:
and all is mossy there.

Our family had moved to the tall red house by the sea when I was ten years old. It was a big house, and, knowing my parents could not afford it, I worried. I worried a lot about grown-ups. To help the house earn its keep, my mother took paying guests. 'Reps', they were called, salesmen who stayed a few nights at a time and were mostly gone by the weekend. Upstairs, the last room along the landing and down two steps, over the kitchen and scullery, was the least grand room on the first floor, my mother's room. My room, the humblest and the highest of all, was above my mother's room, under the roof at the top of a steep flight of stairs. My window looked over the back yard, the bins and the coal shed, and beyond that the vegetable garden, outhouses, the backs of houses in the next road, and, between their roofs, glimpses of the sea. To reach my attic room I raced as fast as I could up the final flight to close my door before a ghost emerged from the door opposite mine. That door led to the loft, a creepy void under the roof-slates, where the water tanks lurked, growling, and the pipes and wires that kept the house-heart beating, and creaking weights that trod the floor and kept me awake and alert on windy nights. No one ever went into the loft, except a plumber or an electrician, or my father fixing something.

Once inside my room, door closed, I was safe, my tree rustling and shimmering outside my window. Over, through and beyond its foliage, over the shoulders of the house-backs in the next road, gleamed the sea. The sound of the sea – too far to hear, but I knew it – was the voice of the tree, as Coleridge's metaphor of the falling, scattering brook lets us see and hear his birch which is, he writes, '… most beautiful of forest trees, the Lady of the Woods'.

Years ago, when we first came to Blaen Cwrt, to remind me of my childhood birch tree and the sound of the sea in its trailing boughs, I had a silver birch planted at the north end of the house in a patch of grassy ground between the gable end and the lane. I hoped that I would see it through the high window over the bookshelves in the study. For years the birch hardly grew. Now, at last, it has grown and spread, reaching its potential to be 'pendulous and fair'. I assume the ground at the house-end is poor and stony, and the tree-roots have spent all their years searching the earth for nourishment. This year, behind the house, about ten yards from the old tree but in a sunnier, more open place, a patch of old pasture, we have planted three young birches. This time the trees were settled more thoughtfully, and already they are flourishing. The sight of them delights me. Of the trees that form the new woodland on our steepest land, over a thousand are sapling birch trees – downy birch – tiny, but now in leaf and bursting from the tubes of their guards.

Betula pendula was one of the first trees to recolonise the land when the last of the Ice Age glaciers melted and retreated. Among the first trees to come into leaf in spring, the birch, *bedwen* in Welsh, is an important tree in Celtic mythology, in legends and fairy stories, a symbol of rebirth. We planted the three trees in a newly acquired patch of land behind the house. Seen through our only west-facing window, which we had inserted in the back wall of the sitting room, their purple-green foliage is the colour of hope.

I have found this quote: 'the silver birch has two hundred and twenty-nine dependent insects while the comparable figures for horse chestnut and sycamore are four and fifteen respectively'. This is cheering news. One of the more frightening reports on the fragile state of the planet warns that insects are in serious decline, their very existence under threat, and, were the world's insects to be wiped out, all living things that depend on them, including we human beings, would die too. I think of bees, of pollination, of crops, of creatures, of the future of our life on earth.

The news is enough to make me pause before I act: how am I going to remove a colony of spiders living between the beams of our bathroom ceiling? The web canopy high above our bed? In the past I might have fetched the vacuum cleaner and hosed the ceiling free. I need a new idea. Perhaps we should collect the spiders in a jam jar, and release them in our big barrel-roofed barn, where nesting swallows will be pleased to see them. They are food for birds, not waste for vacuum cleaners. Besides, they are beautiful. These days I try harder to remove rather than kill creatures as I did in my wasp-swatting, fly-vacuuming, slug-squashing days. A while ago, seeing a tiny luminous creature, a speck of light too small to discern legs, wings, or any part at all, hovering above the black granite surface in the kitchen which I was wiping clean, I wrote these eight lines.

Insect

Over the black granite worktop
where I polish the fossilised dead,
a creature too small to discern
dances on shimmering wings.

Don't set down a plate, a pot
till it's safely flown.
Don't let the light of the world be less
by a single glimmering thing.

By the time it was written, the insect had flown. It was so small, and in motion, a tiny whirr of light, so I could not observe it closely enough to describe it to a friend in the Insect Department at the Museum of Zoology in Cambridge. I wanted an identification, a name, but he was too much of a professional to make a guess. I wished I could name my insect, and learn of its place in the natural order of the world. Because it lived, it would breed, and reproduce its kind. Enough, I suppose.

An old hazel grows in the garden close to the drive, its neighbour a huge laburnum. One end of our washing line is attached to the hazel, the other end is tied to an old plum tree, the last surviving tree of Marged's old orchard. It is a shapeless old plum, but it fruits every year, and the hazel regularly produces nuts. Hazel saplings have been planted as a hedge on the bank raised between our newly acquired piece of land and Allt Maen - the farm next door - and, out of sight, on the slopes, six hundred and forty-five hazel saplings are beginning to dream a wood. It is the third smallest group in the new plantation, so that number is a guess, but I like to think of it, to say that number, to say its name. Dormice will be glad.

The new wood will have six hundred and forty-five rowan trees, the same number as of hazels. Rowan. The 'Mountain Ash', named for its narrow, ash-like leaves and its ability to flourish on high ground. It is the ash of the traditional Welsh song, 'The Ash Grove'. It is also known as the Witch Tree, because a rowan at the gate keeps witches away. Indeed there is an old rowan planted not far from our gate, no doubt by Marged's grandfather sometime in the nineteenth century, and never has a witch dared enter. I am glad to imagine a tree busy warning off witches, although for me it is enough to know that there will be six hundred and forty-five beautiful trees, lanceolate-leafed, lit with white blossoms in spring and clusters of scarlet berries in autumn. A glory to look forward to as the year darkens.

The birds and I anticipate the first autumn of fruiting wild cherries, *prunus avium*. Will they blossom in their first spring, as the cherries planted in the hedges along our borders with Pant Swllt? As time passes, I hope to see them begin their great journey to the sky – mature cherry trees can grow to thirty metres, and live for sixty years. In the meantime, in spring the nectar and pollen will please the bees, in autumn, blackbirds and song thrushes will eat the fruits and scatter the stones to seed more trees, and badgers, wood mice and dormice will feed on fallen fruit. Cherries shelter many caterpillars: cherry fruit moths, cherry bark moths, the orchard ermine, the brimstone and short-cloaked moth. The names are poetry!

March 2020

On 9 March, we were guests in the Senedd for an event to mark the First World War centenary, maybe our last event away from home for a while. Things are getting serious, Mark Drakeford and I and others bumped elbows instead of shaking hands. Now all the talk is of coronavirus and financial collapse.

Thursday 12 March

Home to Blaen Cwrt, empty roads, clean air, silence. Our woods grow silently.

An Oak Wood and an Ancient Bog
April 2018

A hare in the gate! Red-gold. Its hot heart beating – I can almost hear it, almost feel the heat of it, settling to stillness in its form behind the acer, between the blue hydrangea and the gap in the hedge. What does it think about, hour after hour? We see its black-tipped ears flicker above the grasses. When it leaves its form for a run we take a look at the still-warm hollow in the earth and crushed grass. I once heard the poet R.S. Thomas say that he believed in God when he put his hand in the empty form of the hare and found it warm, like a room someone just left. The hare comes and goes. Today it ran across the terrace, nibbled parsley in the old ceramic sink planted with herbs, knocked over a watering can, bounded over the lawn and through the gap. It does not give a damn! It has no need to consider its beauty, strength, agility, speed. It leaves that to me. Every day, its ears pierce the grass, spear-still. I pass close by, say 'Hello, Hare!' as I walk past. It doesn't flinch or blink. Its eye is a planet. It accepts our presence. We are no threat to the fastest runner we know. We are no more than animals who live on the same bit of land. We have our tracks through the grass, and the hare has its own.

April 2019

In the first week of April, 2019, I hear the clatter of a machine working Pant Swllt's field, beyond the hedge at the end of Cae Blaen Cwrt. Clouds of earth-dust rise. They are ploughing. I think of Thomas Hardy's poem, 'In Time of "The Breaking of Nations"'. It speaks to the broken times in which we live:

Only a man harrowing clods
In a slow silent walk
With an old horse that stumbles and nods
Half asleep as they stalk.

Only thin smoke without flame
From the heaps of couch-grass;
Yet this will go onward the same
Though Dynasties pass.[1]

Of course, these days our neighbour's plough is pulled by a huge tractor, not a stumbling, nodding old horse, but it rattles over the field, harrowing clods, clouds of red dust rising under flights of gulls, kites and crows which eye the disturbed earth for worms, as they have always done, since days when the sod was turned by the plough.

It is not so many years since horse-drawn ploughs still worked fields difficult to reach. Seamus Heaney's poem, 'Follower', remembers his father ploughing with a horse, and I recall, as a child staying with Ga, (my *mamgu*, grandmother) on the farm in Pembrokeshire, being hoisted by Gwylim, who worked the farm for Ga, onto a big, gentle carthorse, and the sound of his hand slapping its beautiful, glossy rump to set it going. Off we went, the horse, like Hardy's, stumbling and nodding its way up the steep shortcut through the wood, its head bowing and rising in a rocking-horse motion, with me clinging to its mane and neck, till we reached the top field where Gwylim and the plough were waiting for us. I was proud of my important job, taking the horse to the top field, although in truth it was the other way about – it was the horse, knowing the way, who took me.

---

1 'In Time of "The Breaking of Nations"', Thomas Hardy.

16 April

The public mood is dark. Britain is divided. A word-wall is being raised across the land, and between us and the rest of Europe. Hard words and fracturing phrases make an ugly lexicon. I can't write such words on my white page. As if we needed a dramatic symbol for such heartbreak, yesterday in Paris, on its island in the Seine, a terrible fire blazed over Paris as Notre Dame Cathedral burned. This morning the magnificent 'forest' of its roof, branching beams, the timber fret and lacework are burnt to ashes. The tower has fallen. The symbolism of such destruction keeps us sleepless for the damage ugly politics and politicians have done to the weave and weft of our European cultural connections, our architecture, literature, music, art, those things which made me, which have made us all whether we know it or not.

Trees are our solace. The planting of our woodland was completed in March, sapling trees over six and a half acres from Cae Bach to the old oak wood. I imagine them covering the hill in a few years' time, and within a decade reaching for the sky, casting 'shadows numberless', sheltering birds, mammals, millions of insects and more every year.

In these broken times it is a comfort to see them, young trees covering the *fronnau,* our slopes. The track takes us across Cae Blaen Cwrt, down the hornbeam avenue, through Cae Bach,[2] a cosy small field around which, when we bought our land years ago, we had the destroyed hedges restored. The hedge-wrecker was a butcher with no understanding of the Welsh hill country. He blundered in, ripped out hedge-banks, upset the neighbours, went bankrupt, and left. The land was confiscated by the bank against the debt, and the neighbour who bought it offered us eighteen acres at the price he had

---

2 small field.

paid for it. We bought it gratefully. Our acreage now includes the south side of the Glowan valley and the two-and-a-half-acre ancient oak wood which floods with bluebells in May. We bought the bluebell wood to save it, and all the fields that led to it.

April is a dream of trees coming into leaf, every bud an unspoken word. Here, in the garden, leaves are unfolding on our two chestnuts, always first. Our pieris is a giant - ten foot high, ten foot broad, its red bracts are flame; the acers are Persian red; one of our two great beech trees is fully green; the other, the cautious one, the larger tree, waits a week or so, as it does every year, as if to be sure it's safe to open. This year they are both leafing far earlier than usual, deceived, I fear, by the freak February 'heatwave'.

The first swallows have arrived. 16 April. Just two so far, but five days earlier than last year. 'In the time of the breaking of nations' I grasp natural signs of hope. It is thrilling to watch the birds swoop over the big shed, rediscovering remembered territory from last year and, maybe, the year before. I assume they are male swallows staking their claim on their remembered piece of earth, their sky. So far there are only two birds diving in and out of the gap over the shed doors and out over the house to circle high above the field. Will more soon follow? There are old nests to survey in the shed and under the house-eaves, before the flock arrives to join them. We usually have dozens, and they produce two, sometimes three broods of fledgelings, so that at summer's end scores of swallows are in the sky trying their wings over the barn, the garden, the land. They nest under the house-eaves too, as well as in the barn. When all our doors are open, they use this room for fly-past displays. In through one glass door and out the other, or on and out through the kitchen door. It is one more reason we can't call our house our own!

19 April, Good Friday

Sorrow in Belfast. A young, gay, woman journalist has been shot dead, it is assumed by a gunman in the New IRA. This is what walls do, religious, cultural, racial, verbal. Walls break Britain with prejudice, whispers and lies. It is what cutting ourselves from our European allies and raising walls inside a divided Ireland does. The day of the Good Friday Agreement, 10 April 1998, after helping a ewe to birth her lambs, I wrote a poem.

A Difficult Birth

An old ewe that somehow till this year
had given the ram the slip. We thought her barren.
Good Friday, and the Irish peace deal close,
and tonight she's serious, restless and hoofing the straw.

We put off the quiet supper and bottle of wine
we'd planned, to celebrate if the news is good.
Her waters broke an hour ago and she's sipped
her own lost salty ocean from the ground.

While they slog it out in Belfast, eight decades
since Easter 1916, exhausted, tamed by pain,
she licks my fingers with a burning tongue,
lies down again. Two hooves and a muzzle.

But the lamb won't come. You phone for help
and step into the lane to watch for car lights.
This is when the whitecoats come to the women,
well meaning, knowing best, with their needles and forceps.
So I ease my fingers in, take the slippery head
in my right hand, two hooves in my left.

We strain together, harder than we dared.
I feel a creak in the limbs and pull till he comes

in a syrupy flood. She drinks him, famished, and you find us
peaceful, at a cradling that might have been a death.
Then the second lamb slips through her opened door,
the stone rolled away.

The stone of prejudice in the heart, the stone in the mouth of the tomb, the stuck head of the lamb I helped to birth. Barriers in hearts and minds shifted. Will they return with Brexit?

On our way to Cardigan I look for 'beechen green', signs of spring leaves in the trees flanking the road. Chestnuts, usually first to leaf, are already greening among their bare neighbours. Next will be oaks, and last, usually, ash trees. Will any ash trees leaf this year? Or are they all lost? Beech trees stand along the roadside, and I see first signs of 'beechen green' on their branches, far sooner than usual.

20 April, Easter Saturday

Mid-afternoon silence. Heat rises. The sky is cloudless. It's the warmest Easter I can remember. I listen from where I write at the table in our oak-frame room, glass doors open wide to the east over the lawn and laburnums, and south to the beech trees. Deprived of his old ash-tree spire, the blackbird sang all morning somewhere south of the garden. I found him perched on a willow that leans over the stream which rises in our garden, first welling as the Llymru, to swell and become the Bwdram as it flows down the valley to join the river Glowan. In the valley, on the slope on our side of the stream, the infant woodland stirs, sap rising, roots wriggling down a little further every day, a pricking in the leaf buds. I sense it, even where no leaf has opened.

The heat grows. Trees hang still. The blackbird falls silent for an hour. A willow warbler, which sang all morning somewhere beyond the beech trees, is quiet now; and closer, louder, a chaffinch sang, and stopped. Their three songs measure space, sounding depth and distance, a horizon of hills. In honour of the chaffinch I had a little bit of bread and some cheese for my lunch. Now, at twenty minutes past three, somewhere among the young leaves of the closest beech tree, the willow warbler takes up his song again. And now the chaffinch too begins. His song is louder, closer, repeating over and over the same refrain, again, again, again. And farther off, the blackbird's aria.

27 April

It is a week after Easter. No more swallows have arrived. Where are they this year? Our ecologist, Alison, reports her expected swallows have not returned. I read that migrating birds are caught in nets in the Mediterranean off the coast of Africa. Terrible, if true.

*

Our granddaughter Mali and her partner Huw have come to visit us and to see the bluebell wood at its finest hour. In the old wood the oak trees stand to their ankles in blue for the last weeks of April into May, British bluebells, *Hyacinthoides non-scripta,* the native species with slender leaves and delicate, drooping heads of bells. The oak-leaves are not yet open, so the wood is flooded with sunlight, and, urged by April's long, light days, the bluebells are in full flower. It's a good bluebell year, the trees standing in a sweet-scented, shimmering flood of blue, violet, purple, the blues of lapis lazuli, of Renoir's *La Parisienne.*

At the far end of the oakwood a hedge-bank marks the border between our land and a neighbour's steep field of grazing cattle. Beyond that field is another wood, where brambles have suffocated the bluebells. In the old days, woods were sometimes used for wintering cattle. Maybe such light, occasional grazing kept our wood clear of brambles. Bluebells grow along the lane at the foot of the slope that marks the southern border of our land, but they can't survive the suffocating darkness of the bramble wood.

*

Mali, Huw and Mina the dog take the track through the fields to the wood, and we follow later in the pickup, bumping over Cae Blaen Cwrt, down the hornbeam avenue, through Cae Bach,[1] past the little copse of larch trees marking the corner where Cae Bach meets Fron Blaen Cwrt,[2] where our new woodland begins. Onward, across the top of Fron Felen, through Cae Delyn[3] and down the track to the oak wood. All the way from the larch wood to the bluebell wood sapling trees are waking on the steep south-facing slopes. As the pickup creeps along the track, scents fill the air: first the coconut smell of gorse, then the cooler, sweeter scent of blue, deepening until we are dizzy with it. It is like a wine tasting. Where the new woodland meets the old wood, where gorse and bramble used to be bluebells are already spreading among the infant trees. I plan to live forever to see bluebell woods cover the whole hillside.

Four humans and one dog stand still and silent on the track, taking it in, every sense alert to the warmth and cool of it, the

---

1 *Cae Bach*: small field.

2 *fron*: slope.

3 *delyn/telyn*: harp.

colour and scent of blue. Below, along the lane, a driver slows his car, pausing to wind down the window to take in scent and colour. The lane runs along our border at the foot of the newly planted slopes, and on the far side of the lane is the land of the farm named Llawr Cwrt. It is flat, 'unimproved' land, never ploughed, occasionally grazed by Welsh Black cattle. Llawr Cwrt contains a Site of Special Scientific Interest, an ancient bog, a 'rhos', known as Rhos Llawr Cwrt.

An oak-and-bluebell wood on a steep, south-facing slope, an ancient bog, separated by the width of a country lane. In ecological terms an Ice Age divides them. In the wetlands of Rhos Llawr Cwrt the ground mainly consists of peat. It is rushy and all but treeless, and deep within the marshland we can see a round pool, blue with reflected sky. The pool is a pingo hole, a deep vacuum filled with meltwater left behind thousands of years ago after the slow, post-glacial thaw. There are many pingo holes on Rhos Llawr Cwrt, though all but the one we can see have silted up over millennia.

'Pingo' is an Inuit word for a mound or ice-bowl, a periglacial landform. At the end of the last Ice Age, the ice remained frozen longest in these deep chambers, slowly melting to leave lakes behind. Gazing down over the bog, considering its story, its aeons of time, reminds me how, as a child lying in bed, I would scare myself thinking of 'forever and ever'. This ancient bog is the very incarnation of forever and ever: preserved, untouched, undrained by farmers, unlike much other similar land. A very special place, once owned – thankfully! – by a neglectful farmer, it is valued by its current owner, and, for the treasure it offers, it is subject to a conservation order and protected by Natural Resources Wales.

Rhos Llawr Cwrt is home to at least one special insect – the marsh fritillary butterfly, which depends for its existence entirely on devil's bit scabious, a wildflower which grows undisturbed on the bog. Other butterflies, dragonflies and damselflies thrive on the Rhos, home to rare plants like the slender green feather moss *(Hamatocaulis vernicosus)*. Harvest mice live in the tussocks of purple moor grass which cover the Rhos, prey to hunting barn owls. The stream which rises in our garden and runs down the valley on the south border of our land flows into the Glowan and through the Rhos. We have seen otters, and signs of otters, along the stream, and once, hearing a night-splash in our pond, torchlight found the freshly skinned skull of a frog, and otter spraint on the bank. We have watched the butterflies crawling over the scabious in the bog, and in 2015, while poet-in-residence at the Museum of Zoology, Cambridge, I saw examples of the species in a glass case, pinned to eternal stillness by a Victorian collector.

Marsh Fritillaries

A drawer of butterflies,
each impaled on the tiny stilt of its pin,
as numerous as those quivering, alive
in the colonies on Cors Llawr Cwrt, larvae
that live on devil's bit scabious on the bog.
They hunger, eat, belong, mate, breed and die.
I love their language, pupae, chrysallis,
the coloured oculi that dot their wings,
their almost symmetry, their beauty
nourished on buttercup, betony, bugle,
sprung from the hoof-prints of grazing cattle
on wetland and marsh.
Though none here stir, they could be alive.
If I gaze long enough, they move.

Rhos Llawr Cwrt has been recorded as the best site in Britain, perhaps in Europe, for this butterfly. How I would love the marsh fritillary to live on our land! But crossing the lane would be an impossible distance for it to travel. Besides, the bog is wet, the peat deep and rich, the terrain treeless, perfect for the devil's bit scabious and its dependent butterfly, as well as other species. Our wood is steep, south-facing, sunlit, its soil well-drained and rich with leaf-mould, ideal for sessile oaks and bluebells, for underground living for an extended family of badgers, for dens for foxes, its trees perfect nesting sites for buzzards, kites and crows.

*

An oak-and-bluebell wood on a steep south-facing slope. A flat, ancient bog. Neighbouring sites divided by a narrow country lane and by aeons of time, each the perfect habitat for its own species of plant, insect, mammal and bird. A wonderful world! But will it live forever and ever? These days it is not 'forever and ever', but its opposite, the fear of extinction, which keeps me awake at night, as does this mysterious question: how did the marsh fritillary butterfly find its way to Rhos Llawr Cwrt, and, in particular, to its patch of devils bit scabious, in the first place?

*

Spring Equinox, 2020

The night summer came to a world remade,
streets were carless, silence walked the roads.
A kite's red-gold, flamboyant,
floated flame on blue,
flexed wings and the fork of his tail
and turned on a breath.

Miles high over the fields,
over flights of rooks, crows, gulls,
over the cities, the clouds, the atmosphere,
in the vault of heaven the ozone layer cleared
of particulates, of nitrogen dioxide,
and we breathed again.

Listen! In this clean new silence
all sound is birdsong,
a small wind in the trees,
the fall of a petal, an opening leaf,
the turn of a page,
your breath, mine.

Ring of Gold
May 2018

The hare is in the garden every day now. It comes and goes from its form by the hedge. A cuckoo calls from somewhere to the south, down in the Glowan valley.

Our May garden is in flower: Michaelmas daisies, sweet cicely, wild geraniums, the laburnum hedge just opening, new bracts on the pieris turning from scarlet to pale gold, wild flowers too many to name. The sea of blue in the oak wood fades as the bluebells fall to seed. All day and every day the blackbird sings, and the thrush repeats his song thrice over, all to the continuing songs of willow warbler, chiffchaff, wren.

Regret at the fading of the bluebells recedes as the buds begin to open on the hedge of wild laburnum that every May holds the garden in its ring of gold. The laburnum is glorious, a hedge of gold between drive and lane, garden and fields, the longhouse almost encircled.

The laburnum hedge had grown unchecked for over a hundred years, so it was with great sorrow that we realised we must breech the ring of gold on the western side, which runs along the blank back wall of the house – blank but for the new window we had inserted into the rear wall of our sitting room. The longhouse was built backed into the hillside as, centuries ago, many such houses were. The field behind rises steeply above the house foundations, and the bank was a house-long bulwark barely two feet from our wall. Our new rear window looked into the darkness of the hedge-bank with its hedge of laburnums grown tall as trees. Not a beam of sunlight got through. A greater problem was the damp that seeped from the higher land into our back wall. We did not own the land behind the house, so we could do nothing. Sitting room and hall, bedroom and study were permanently damp. Until we bought the corner of Allt Maen's big field, nothing could be done.

The laburnums are beautiful, and I loved seeing the unbroken ring of gold every May, but six trees behind the house had to go. A neighbour, Arfon, working the huge shovel of his digger with precision and delicacy, took out the trees and the bank, made a shallow slope further back, and levelled the land above. Now sun pours in, warms the rear house wall, and Blaen Cwrt has a back garden. The old longhouse is set free. It seems to breathe, settled in its new space. The back wall, which we have never seen before, basks in air and sunlight. South-western light pours over the south terrace and into the house through the new sitting-room window. The rear wall has dried out after crouching for almost two centuries in damp and darkness.

1 May 2019

These days I have two artists on my mind: Leonardo da Vinci, painter, inventor, thinker, engineer, in his fifth centenary year, and David Nash, artist, sculptor, tree and wood lover. We attended the opening of his exhibition in the National Museum in Cardiff. I love his trees, his work, his wood, his circular ash grove growing in a secret place somewhere in Snowdonia. Trees on my mind, I think of Edward Thomas's cherry trees, our infant cherries in bud:

> The cherry trees bend over and are shedding
> On the old road where all that passed are dead,
> Their petals, strewing the grass as for a wedding
> This early May morn where there is none to wed.

Commissioned to write a poem for Leonardo da Vinci's quincentenary, I am rereading my old Art A-level books, the Renaissance, from Giotto to da Vinci. My poem will be set by composer and friend Adrian Williams for Robert

Hollingworth's choir, I Fagiolini. Trying to understand gravity, long before it was understood or named, Leonardo set something rolling down a hill, and watched its accelerating speed, its gradual slowing to a stop as the ground levelled. He imagined sound waves, long before they had been discovered. He longed to solve the mystery of flight. In the poem I see him alone in the hospital at night, dissecting a bat, taking apart the bones of its wings for their engineering, their structure. He sought to understand its secret, how the creature could fly on invisible waves on the air. He forecast: 'creatures of the earth shall mount up among the stars. Men from the most remote countries shall speak to one another, and shall reply'.

Sounding

Listen! Bats on the evening air
sounding the dusk with cries too high to hear,
invisible scribbles on the sky. One fell,
broken, a heartbeat in the palm of your hand.
You probed its bones for the mystery of flight.
In your theorem's thrumming drum of certainty.
Before physics, before the miracle had a name,
you knew we'd free ourselves from gravity's shackles,
break the chains that hold us to the ground,
loose the weight of footfall, foothold
for the hush and lift of air beneath our wings,
to lift and fly as arrows, shooting stars.

And before we knew long wave, how sound can ride
up, up to touch the ionosphere and return,
you foretold we'd speak over oceans
like bats in the evening sky, and you knew,
seeking the secret of flight in its engineered bones,
how we would lift ourselves on the same air.

*

We flew to Dublin, where Colm and Orlagh met us at the airport and drove us all the straight way to Strokestown for the festival, for a glorious weekend of poetry with a warm Irish audience. They appreciated my little blue flag with its circle of gold stars, placed on the lectern as I opened my book to read. Lovely poets, Paddy Bushe, Jane Clarke, James Harpur, Enda Wyley, and so many others to read alongside, listen to, and share the *craic*. Paddy invited me to the festival next year in County Kerry. It's like being back in the heart of an unbroken Europe. Wales and Ireland have much in common, much to share.

*

Home to find, after those few warm, sweet days, May has turned bitter cold. A swooping curve from the north in an Atlantic weather front has brought in an Arctic ice-wind to bite us. I worry for the tender leaves that opened too soon on some trees, especially the beech. Urged into leaf by a freak February heatwave, now bitten by a winter wind in May.

What is happening to the seasons? January brings the snow, February brings the rain, the winds of March, April showers, May flowers… and so on.

*

My favourite summer singer is the blackbird, as sweet as Keats's nightingale, which:

in some melodious plot
Of beechen green and shadows numberless
Singest of summer in full-throated ease

But this year, 'beechen green', that tenderest, freshest of all the greens of early summer, is destroyed, scorched by an ice-wind. Under the red acer, burnt leaves scatter the lawn like a shadow, all west-facing bracts on the pieris are brown, and on the west side of our two great beech trees all tender new foliage is scorched, shrivelled, dead. Now that summer evenings are here, the hedge-bank removed and the terrace open to all the light of the westering sun, we are ready for a first outdoor sip, then supper, with a wood-fire in the belly of our 'Iron Man', if we need warming as the sun declines.

One of my greatest early summer pleasures was to sit with my back to the setting sun, and to gaze into the cool of our beech trees 'beechen green', spring's tenderest colour. I could almost taste it. But not a leaf has survived. Our beautiful trees are withered and shrivelled. I don't recall this ever happening before this year.

11 May

Summer. After hours working in the garden David drove us along the lane below the oak wood on the way to see Clinton at Coed y Cardi to talk about timber cladding for the little studio/guest room David is building. As we arrived he said, 'This bit of Ceredigion is so beautiful.' It is true. Waiting in the pickup, I looked over the fields towards the tree-lined road into Talgarreg. David reminded me that the landowner had begun to fell those trees, but he did not get far before our neighbour from Pant Swllt told him he should stop, as the villagers were upset to see such destruction. Thank God the man listened. Broken boughs scar the row, but the treeline stands, and will heal.

*

Our overland track to the wood, fenced and cleared of gorse, is now easier to walk, and Alison, from the forestry company, tells us that a man will soon be working on the land in the early mornings to spray and clear bramble regrowth among the saplings. Below the wood, all along the lane, the chestnuts are in leaf, forming a green tunnel all the way to our furthest gateway where, a few weeks ago, we parked and walked the track, breathed the scent of bluebells, and gloried in the view over Llawr Cwrt bog to the hills beyond.

The heat rises. Birdsong. Glass doors open for the messages of willow warbler, chaffinch, blackbird, and innumerable, more distant choristers. I work in the cool of this room, David in the study – the old *beudy*, five rooms along at the end of the house – then out to sip and sup together on the sunny terrace as the sun dips westwards. Wild laburnum is about to break into flower about the fields, *tresi aur*, golden chains. The almost-circle of the hedge is weighed with unopened buds. Apart from the opened space behind the house, a loop of waterfalling gold is about to break into flower to the north, east and south. Laburnums surround many fields and borders and grow along many of the lanes in Ceredigion. It is a local wonder that is not, as far as I know, seen anywhere else in Britain. All over rural Ceredigion, we see fields hedged with gold, and many lanes and main roads, including much of the A487 to Cardigan, are a golden road every May. Planted early in the last century, by now they are hedgerow trees for which the area is famous. How did they happen? How did such a feature get here? One cannot imagine a Ceredigion farmer, certainly not in those hard old days, when scraping a living from the land was so tough, deliberately marking the borders of his fields with a beautiful, poisonous tree which more usually graced grand gardens. As the story goes, a travelling salesman sold fencing stakes to farmers early in the last century. They proved to be living fence posts, and one long-ago spring, up and down Ceredigion, they rooted and broke into leaf. By now, over a century later, they are great trees, multi-stemmed, tall and spreading. Around our house and garden, where long ago an old man scraped a living with his daughter and granddaughter, they form a ring of gold. Despite their toxic seeds, we have never heard of a case of cattle poisoning. Animals know better than to eat them.

This continuum of trees, birds, beauty, the balance of things, eases anxiety over the chaos of British and world politics. As I write, water-light dances on the ceiling when a breeze stirs the sunlit surface of the moat that runs along the two glass walls. It is murky green-brown when I gaze into it, yet it casts crystal-clear light on the ceiling.

13 May

Along the lane in the pickup, we drive onto our land through our bottom gate and park below the oak wood, above Rhos Llawr Cwrt. We watch a hare run the fields below. The past year has been a good one for hares, and our neighbours report that hare numbers are increasing here. The young hare which made a form in our garden last year returned to it every day until winter. This March two hares chased each other across the lawn and through the gate into Cae Blaen Cwrt. Was 'our' hare one of them?

17 May

A week of summer, warm, still, cloudless, and the laburnum – golden chain, *tresi aur* – is in full flower, trailing its heavy tresses with no wind to stir them, and the scent is glorious. These days the room which was once the *parlwr*[1] is our bathroom. It is one of life's luxuries to lie in the bath contemplating the waterfallling light of the huge laburnum outside the bathroom window. That particular tree towers above the house, many-stemmed and wide-spreading, its silver-green interleaving with a neighbouring hazel's gold-green foliage. As well as encircling the garden, laburnums form an arcade over the drive and our parked car. In June, as the flowers fade, the fallling petals of *tresi aur* will gild the car.

This year, before the flowers opened, from that same little window I watched a pair of magpies build their nest high in the branches of one of the laburnums. One bird dropped a small twig, then followed it down, hopping branch by branch to the ground, recovered it and fluttered up the stairway of the tree to restore the twig to its place in the new nest. In later weeks, as the trees began to flower, I watched the magpie fly to and fro carrying food to its mate on the nest. What must it be like for nestlings to hatch in a house of gold? The hedges reach their peak around our garden, along the lanes, about the fields, slowly opening until, over a few weeks, Ceredigion glows in their full-blown glory, holding their peak of gold a week or two before the first flower falls. I don't want to lose a single day of this sight.

*

I have just thrown a bruised apple onto the lawn, a red fruit in the sunshine. The magpie is there in a black and white flash. Magpies have never been among my favourite birds. I had judged them to be the harsh-voiced bullies of the garden, egg-thieving enemies of other nesting birds. Yet, observing

---

1 parlour.

the tender care the pair took nest-building in the golden tree, their subsequent concern for each other and their eggs, then the young in their nest of sticks, and now this bird's jumping pleasure at the sight of a rotten apple on the lawn in the evening sun, I am won over. The magpie knows the Welsh proverb: 'A seed hidden in the heart of an apple is an orchard invisible.'

18 May

A swarm of bees decided to build a palace of wax in the roof-space over our bedroom. We had noticed them outside, flying in and out of a gap where the roof-ridge meets the wall at the pine-end of the house. One day a crowd of them emerged into the bedroom to buzz at the sun-dazzled glass of our two unopenable roof lights. We decided to wait to see how they would solve their problem, and ours. By nightfall they had returned to their hive in the roof, and all was quiet, the room and roof lights clear. We assume the hive is now complete, all bees accommodated, and their route to and fro between flowers and the honeycomb is settled. Today there was not one bee in the house.

Bees are civilised. Their hive is a city, governed and orderly. I imagine them filling every cell of the comb with gold, each brimming hexagonal cup in their citadel of wax tasting of bluebells and laburnum, with a hint of sweet cicely, azalea, wild roses, Welsh poppies, dandelions. One of my favourite books is the Belgian poet Maurice Maeterlinck's *The Life of the Bee*. As he says of the bee's extraordinary civilisation:

> We might be in one of the castles of German legend, whose walls are composed of myriad phials containing the souls of men about

> to be born. For we are in the abode of life that goes before life. On all sides asleep in their closely sealed cradles, in this infinite superposition of marvellous six-sided cells, lie thousands of nymphs, whiter than milk, who, with folded arms and head bent forward await the hour of awakening. In their uniform tombs that, isolated, become nearly transparent, they seem almost like hoary gnomes lost in deep thought, or legions of virgins whom the folds of the shroud have contorted, who are buried in hexagonal prisms that some inflexible geometrician has multiplied to the verge of delirium… and in the midst of this growing world that so soon shall transform itself, that shall four or five times in succession assume fresh vestments, and then spin its own winding-sheet in the shadow, hundreds of workers are dancing, and flapping their wings.'

Falling asleep under the roof where they sought refuge, imagining the bees in their castle, I recall the lines in 'The Laws of Hywel Dda':[1]

> the lineage of bees is from paradise and it was because of man's sin that they came from there and that God gave them his grace; and therefore the mass cannot be sung without the wax.

Later, when the last bee had left our room and gone home, David found one that had been caught in a cobweb. He carefully carried it to the table on a sheet of paper, and fetched a pair of tweezers from the bathroom. While he delicately held parts of the cobweb with the tweezers, I drew each thread away. At last, when web and bee were untangled, and David deemed the creature safe to clean itself of the little that remained, he stepped onto the terrace and set it free. It reminded me of the hour we spent cutting a robin free from fruit-bush netting. Should I now write a poem called 'How to Mend a Bee'?

---

1 twelfth century.

22 May

The hare has come home to our garden. Chased from her form in Henbant's field where the mower had cut and turned the grass, she ran into the garden using her old route across the terrace, nibbled a flower, then loped onto the stretch of stony earth behind Blaen Cwrt. She returned in the evening to graze the long grass by the fence, as we sipped in the sunshine on the terrace. We hope to have a hare-in-residence once more this year.

27 May, Bank Holiday Monday

After weeks of warm, still days, it is cooler and the wind is rising. In our absence – two days spent travelling to Festivals in Hay and Beaumaris – the laburnum reached full bloom, held a while before it began to fall. In one single long summer day, leaving Gŵyl y Gelli – the Festival in Hay-on-Wye – in the morning, we drove a hundred and forty miles through the mountains of mid-Wales to Beaumaris Festival in Anglesey, where, after an afternoon gig before an appreciative audience, we drove a hundred miles home to Ceredigion. For the whole beautiful journey between distant blue mountains and closer, sunlit slopes and shadow-valleys, the winding road led us between mile after mile of hedgerows foaming with white blossom: cherry, elder, hawthorn, blackthorn, rowan. Some of the species we see in our new woodland. Next May, will the young wild cherries in our woods have grown enough to foam with spring blossom? For now, just to see one new leaf unfurling is enough to reassure me that blossom will follow on the reaching branches of our young sessile oaks, downy birch, rowan, hazel, and the wild cherry trees. They will heal our annual regret at the fade and fall of laburnum.

May 2020

The laburnum circles us with gold. The young cherries leafed, and blossomed, but so did Covid-19. Covid, *corvid* the crow, the whole world its battlefield, picking off the old and the weak. Some of the young too. The grief is terrible.

All gigs are cancelled for the foreseeable future. Hay, Tŷ Newydd, Charleston, Cambridge where I was asked to talk on the poetry of Rowan Williams, and my earned income with it.

I have savings, work to do, time – time to read, time to write. I have three books in progress. My version of 'Y Gododdin' poems, prose essays, and poems when they come, keep me busy. Aid is promised for the self-employed. We will manage. I transferred a sum from my ISA to my current account. David is busy with architecture, and gardening. I love not going anywhere. No motorways, no trains, no planes.

The May weather is glorious, and there is time and silence to relish the garden, tea on the Orchard Lawn, supper and a glass of wine on the terrace.

7 May

A supermoon, closer and seeming larger than any seen for years, rising like a warning beyond the beech trees, lighting the night.

June 2018

A Sky Tree – An Avenue

As May tilts into June the land's on fire,
farms folded deeper into rings
of wild laburnum, *tresi aur*,
fields gold-encircled, the summer air
yellow with yeasty leavening.
Step out. Inhale its musk
in evening's lengthening light
when other colours have dissolved in dusk.

Dark will follow this delicious hour.
In a week the drive, sills, roof, gutters
will be inlaid gold with fallen flowers,
tresses turned to sour rosaries,
poisonous pods ignored by grazing herds.
Relish, before the blackbird's nest is cold,
and he sings no more in the ash,
and we've spent the gold.

The first day of June. Fallen petals gild the car parked in the drive under the big laburnum, with the magpies' nest in its topmost branches. There is a split at the base of the tree between the multiple stems, where the branches rise and divide to north and south. We keep an eye on it – I could not bear to see it fall, or to have it felled. I know a multi-stemmed 'tree' should be called a shrub, but it is tall and spreading.

When we first bought Blaen Cwrt, and for the almost five decades since, an old horse chestnut tree grew out of a wall-bank close to the house, draping the house wall and roof with its shadow. Sprung, we suppose, from the chance fall of a prickly chestnut husk, cracked open well over a hundred years ago to release a ripe nut. The nut, its seed, a conker, fell between the stones, and put its roots down into the rubble. Half of the chestnut's roots had grown into the poor soil between the stones close to the end of the bank, and half had managed to reach down into the richer soil of the grassy floor beyond. So the tree grew slant, inclined to the south. Just a few feet from the house front, it towered over the roof, and no sunlight ever reached the house wall to dry it and clear the mould. All images of Blaen Cwrt, children's drawings and photographs, show the old chestnut tree. Despite its poor position and its shrouding shadow, we never considered felling it.

The trunk was close enough to the kitchen window – once the old dairy – to let us watch a treecreeper, a tiny mottled brown bird, as it descended the chestnut, pecking as it went, feeding on insects that lived in the bark. We often saw a nuthatch too, a beautiful, blue-backed, rose-breasted little bird creeping the bark, relishing insects that feed on decay. The birds knew the chestnut was dying long before we did, as they fed on insects in the crevices of its rotting bark.

Long ago, maybe the early nineteenth century, when the longhouse was raised from the stones of the field, in common with many old Ceredigion smallholdings a wall was built parallel to the front of the house to separate the domestic space from the farmyard, and keep out the stock. About four feet high and four feet deep, our wall, set north to south, was made of thin stones of shale set slant like pages, not much better than rubble. In areas of good local stone such walls were built of strong, cut blocks, packed tight together, rain-and-wind-washed and kept clear of weeds. Our wall of Ceredigion shale collected soil, detritus, fallen leaves, insects and their droppings, and was soon overgrown. By now it has become a beautiful bank of grass and wild flowers: first flowers to open are the snowdrops, then wild daffodils and crocuses, and later primroses, cowslips, violets, dandelions, the poor soil perfect for keeping grass from overwhelming them. On the far side of the wall a few plum trees and a sour old apple tree grew, where long ago, I imagine, hens pecked, and the house pig snouted the earth for whatever it could find.

Beyond the bank, of Marged's little orchard just one plum tree survives, leaning and shapeless, still producing its small, dark-purple fruit. Our washing line is strung between it and a hazel. Along the house front, between the bank and the house, runs the path once used by Marged, her aunt and her grandfather to bear buckets of milk from the *beudy*[1] at the north end to the *llaithdy*[2] on the south. Today their old rubble-and-cinder path is a slate-paved terrace leading from the drive to the front door, and along to the porch built against our kitchen. At its north end the bank turns the corner east, an arm sheltering the old orchard from our drive; at the south end grew the chestnut, children's 'sky tree', low-branched, many-forked and easy to climb. They spent hours in its branches.

A few years ago, showing signs of disease, the chestnut tree left us no choice. Our neighbour, Lloyd, was first to notice our tree was sick. The sky tree had to be felled. There is a horse chestnut disease doing its destructive work all over Britain. A few years ago I saw evidence of this from the window of a train. Every tree along the track bore brown, shrivelled leaves, the sign of dieback. We hoped for the best for our tree, but eventually we called in a neighbouring tree surgeon. He felled it for us. I watched, half-sad to lose an old friend, half-glad to set the house free of its shadow. Nothing can live forever, even a tree.

It is an awesome sight to watch a great tree fall. First Rob the tree man attached a sling to the trunk, and, leaning back in the sling, chainsawed the spreading branches. Then he cut a

---

1 cowshed.

2 dairy.

deep notch in the base of the trunk to control the direction of the tree's fall. We held our breath. At the final cut, it dropped, perfectly judged, away from the house, clear of the plum tree and across the open grass.

It lay in state on the lawn for a few days, then David set to work sawing and chopping it for firewood. Our chestnut kept us warm throughout the following winter, and longer.

What remained rooted into the earth where it had grown was like a giant chair, the 'seat' and back hacked away and sawn as far as the wall-bank allowed, the age-rings too wounded by the axe for us to count them. It is eight years since the tree was felled, and the giant 'chair' survived for years. This year at last it is rotting away, the sky tree gone, its decayed old root feeding nourishment back into the earth.

We miss the treecreeper and the nuthatch who fed on the bark, but once the shade was lifted from the house wall, sunlight bleached away the mould. From autumn the nuthatch comes to the bird feeder, but which tree does it haunt now the chestnut's gone?

*

It was sad to see the tree go, but our urge to plant new trees is greater for its loss. When, years ago, before we had the chance to buy our eighteen acres, a man with no knowledge of or concern for the Welsh hill country, bought a farm across the valley, acquired all our former neighbours' fields to the east, north and south of Blaen Cwrt, to add to his already considerable acreage. He grubbed up hedges and felled trees to create unhindered space, the better for his vast machines to be driven over land unimpeded. Only gorse hedges survived.

His demolition work made us fearful for the ancient oak-and-bluebell wood half a mile away that had so far survived the rampage. We tried to buy some land from him. At first he agreed, then turned angry and refused. He quarrelled with his neighbours, went bankrupt, and departed. The land was bought from the bank by a neighbour, who offered us the piece we wanted for the price he had paid. It extended from Blaen Cwrt to the oak-and-bluebell wood. Dear reader, we bought it!

*

That was over twenty years ago. The way to the oak wood from Blaen Cwrt crosses five fields, or four fields and a strip: Cae[1] Blaen Cwrt; Cae Bach;[2] Fron Blaen Cwrt; Fron Felen;[3] and 'the Ride', as we call it, a sliver of our good neighbour's field, a hundred yards long, about five yards wide, which runs between Cae Blaen Cwrt – our home field – and Cae Bach, allowing us to walk or drive a tractor all the way to the oak wood. Too narrow to be a field, it was the link between the home field and the rest of the acquired land, including our precious wood.

Our first task was to restore destroyed hedges. A neighbour, a tree man, replanted the field borders with native tree and shrub species. In a few years they had grown dense, giving shelter for nesting birds, loud with song spring to midsummer. Cae Bach slopes south, and within two seasons the new trees had flourished around it, leafed, flowered and fruited, making a cosy, sheltered field for new lambs, and hedgerows dense for birds' nests.

What could we do with the sliver of grassland, neither track nor field, that ran between Cae Blaen Cwrt and Cae Bach? We stood at one end looking along it. An avenue, we thought, or a ride. Both names seemed too grand for a few hundred yards of grass with the home field at one end and Cae Bach at the other.

---

1 field.

2 small field.

3 golden slope.

A friend teasingly pointed out that, looking north, the most striking feature framed by our 'avenue' would be our big barrel-roofed shed, and the polytunnel. Hardly ideal features to satisfy a need for a culmination to the view through trees we imagined, their branches touching overhead. But we wanted an avenue, so, in December 1999, as the century turned, as our birthday gift to the planet we had twenty-four hornbeams planted, twelve trees on each side. Immediately, the young trees just slender stems six or eight feet high, they cast their slanting shadows across the grass and created parallels to please the eye and tempt the walker.

Twenty years on they are grown trees. They touch overhead to form an aisle and cast parallel shadows on summer grass, or winter snow. We don't see the barrel-roofed barn for the loveliness of those arching trees, by now interlacing their branches overhead, and their shadows underfoot.

To protect the young trees from prevailing winds that sweep in from high, hedgeless farmland to the west, we planted a new border hedge along the length of the Ride, and beween it and the hornbeams, a sheltering grove of various trees – willows, rowan, a sweet chestnut, a lime – all the way to where an old oak tree at the gate to Cae Blaen Cwrt marks the end of the Ride. Under the trees we planted wild daffodils.

The sheep love the avenue, and the grove. They shelter there from the heat of the sun. They keep the grass short, and have no taste for daffodils. I was once told by a conservationist that hornbeams and beech trees are not native species to Ceredigion. As a result, at the time, some of our old hedges were not considered to be appropriate for a conservation grant. However, a conservationist friend from Yorkshire showed me research that records evidence of beech trees growing in West Wales since soon after the last Ice Age. Indeed, beech grows everywhere here, flourishing all over Ceredigion at the borders of fields and along roads. And why not hornbeam now too?

The climate is changing. Don't we need to extend the range of our native trees, as conditions allow?

June 2019

Flaming June. Warm, sweet days. Long, light evenings. I can't bear to leave Blaen Cwrt at a time like this, when it seems 'warm days will never cease'. Although, in his poem, Keats is not describing June, but a beautiful autumn long ago, before we ruined the climate, his words come to me in this lovely June moment, in anticipation of September.

> And still more, later flowers for the bees,
> Until they think warm days will never cease,
> For Summer has o'er-brimm'd their clammy cells.

6 June

The seventy-fifth anniversary of D-Day. I still remember the day, though not for its famous history. It was two days before my seventh birthday, and my mother was making me a new party dress to wear for my birthday. She had been busy working for days on her Singer sewing machine to finish the dress in time, her two hands feeding the red and blue taffeta with a thin stripe of white under its steadying foot and the dancing needle. Goodness knows where she got it, at a time when necessities were short, never mind taffeta. New clothes were made from old clothes. Old jumpers were unravelled to knit new ones. I remember my sister, three years old, screaming as she paddled in the sea when her home-knitted swimsuit, dragged down by water, left her naked at the edge of the tide.

So my dress, cut from a roll of red, blue and white taffeta, seemed like a party drees from fairy stories. Rags to riches. Cinderella when her dream came true. I was so excited that it was hard not to wriggle as my mother dropped the dress over my head, impaling me with the pins which still held it together.

Once she had finished with me, I went to bed in the small room over the front porch, in our house in Barry, too excited to sleep, my blue and white curtains drawn, a 'blackout' curtain beneath, I suppose, so that not a chink of light would escape to tempt Hitler to drop his bombs on us. Even on a June evening, the room was dark.

We did not know it then, but it would be a date that made history. I often wondered if my father, through his work at the BBC, had wind of something significant afoot. I fell asleep, to be woken hours later when he came into my room, lifted me from my bed onto the windowsill and drew back the curtains to show the night sky, where plane after plane was roaring south over Barry. There seemed to be hundreds of them. And he said: 'Never forget this sight.' Or did he say, 'never forget this night'?

I did forget, until, years later, on holiday during my birthday week, as David and I drove from the ferry port through northern France. Flags were flying along the roadsides, in gardens, on flagpoles, on house tops and from windows. French, American and British flags, marking a celebration, the sixtieth anniversary of D-Day. A revelation! In a flash of memory I recalled that night long ago, held in my father's arms on the windowsill of my room in Barry, sleepy but excited at the thought of my imminent birthday, the sky roaring with planes, and his words. My birthday party, the taffeta dress cut to a paper pattern, the pins, the song of the Singer, the sky loud with the thrum of the planes, the secretive rustle of paper, and at last a candle-lit cake, had swept away the great historic moment, to survive, lost and found a lifetime later in what Yeats describes as the 'rag and bone shop of the heart'.

7 June

At breakfast, as rain fell steadily, tapping the terrace, we saw a sweet sight: a young magpie, its feathers dirty and dishevelled, perched on a bucket under the slate table, shaking the rain from its plumage. It shook, shook and settled there gazing at the wet world. Clever bird! Later, as rain fell steadily all day, it returned, hunched, occasionally shaking itself. It was still there in the evening when we withdrew to the sitting room, and the glow of the wood-burning stove.

8 June

A bright, warm day, with passing showers, the trees singing. David made me scrambled eggs and smoked salmon for lunch. We sipped after supper, until the sun went down. A lovely birthday.

9 June

Sunday, the day after my birthday, Cai, our eldest grandson, and his partner Eliza, visiting from Australia, arrived with Llaima and Huw for my birthday lunch. A day late, but two birthdays are better than one. The very first thing Cai said, as he saw the space where the sky tree used to be, was 'Where has my tree gone?' It's been a few years since he came to Blaen Cwrt.

11 June

Work done, the Alpine Foundation Award almost decided between me and John Burnside, and last night, as we slowly sipped the dregs of the glass and the day, my reward was a beautiful visitor: Hare! This time, soaked by a heavy shower, it paused on the mown grass in the hedge-gap between the garden and the Middle Lawn, and spent perhaps half an hour cleaning its hind feet, a meticulous, energetic job which let us observe in detail its white underfur and its glorious eye, its black ears, as it shook its head free of drops, its red-brown fur shaken and smoothed until at last, comfortable in its own furry skin, it loped away into the long grass and under the beech beyond the bank. Such a privilege to watch so intimate an act, an animal cleaning its self and its soul. Such sweet distraction from the wound of broken Britain.

20 June

Midsummer Eve. I must write a poem before the blackbird stops singing for another season, must write it for Keats, my tribute to his 'Ode to a Nightingale', for the anthology of tribute poems by the Keats-Shelley Association. A cloudless, beautiful day to work on it.

Ode to a Blackbird

Midsummer morning, he sings his Latin
six-syllable refrain again again,
psalm of possession in your beechen green.
Doors open to the day, I listen. His bell's
as sweet, dear Poet, as your nightingale,
the voice of summer. Windless. Almost still.

A slight stir as the beech trees' open hands
combing the sky, loosen airy strands
of cirrus cloud on blue. He understands
the garden's his. We sing to hold our ground
in the shadowy woodlands of the mind;
the blackbird's calling to our kind.
We rhyme
to mark our place in time.

*

The hare is here every day. Yesterday it loped across the terrace, nibbled a dandelion, tried some parsley, and ran away over the terrace to the south. The sun is high. Small white clouds float like yachts on blue. Water-light dances on the ceiling. I am trying to read, think, find song in language, distraction from the tricks and deceits of a new, ugly politics.

The garden heals us. Summer roses. 'Albertine' is in bloom. 'Celestial' is opening, as are the multiplying yellow flowers of 'Hidcote' in the bed across the lawn.

After lunch, a shower of rain, the blackbird sings with a drop of rain in his throat. Hare crosses the terrace. David comes in, reporting a cream-spot tiger butterfy, and five orchids in Cae Blaen Cwrt. June flames to a close in all its beauty, despite disheartening news of the worst political situation I have ever known. How can we continue to feel so sad, so worried, so angry as the long light of evening offers us such beauty? Is this what beauty is for?

June 2020

I sent *Y Gododdin* to Faber on the first of June. Light in the dark. A flight of crows darkens the fields, scavenging for flesh. Corvids, Covid, their shadows the darkness of Brexit-and-Boris-Broken Britain. When will it end? When will the old life return?

Beechen Green and Shadows Numberless
July 2018

The first of July… and on the hour the blackbird stops singing. He knows the date. His work is done. Maybe, if it rains, he will sing this evening with a water-drop in his throat. Maybe once more tomorrow. I am commissioned to write a poem for Keats, whose nightingale sang 'in beechen green and shadows numberless'. As my tribute, I will give John Keats an 'Ode to a Blackbird', whose aria has sounded from our beechen green, dawn to dusk since early spring, and will again, we hope, next year. It is my favourite song. My Desert Island Disc.

The BBC weather map shows a mass of rain-bearing cloud close by, ink-blue, yellow-hearted, green-haloed. Enough to recharge the tanks, the moat, to drench the garden and get the grass growing again. I wish for a hush of rain, long, slow and quenching. A bird is singing, but it's not the blackbird. Swallows are swooping over the house. A red kite sails slowly overhead, each wing and both forks of its tail flexing separately. I don't know another bird that can do this. A few butterflies are blown on a light wind. We can see a cloud, but it does not look rain-loaded. A harbinger perhaps.

8pm. Rain! Real rain, not a storm, but sweet, steady rain, plucking the roof like a harp, singing the grateful garden back to life. I swear I hear the beech trees drinking. But the blackbird is silent.

2 July

The rain came and went. The heatwave goes on and on. Lunch and supper on the terrace every day. This could be France.

Wednesday, 4 July

The seventieth birthday of the NHS, and I read my commissioned poem at the memorial service in Llandaff Cathedral. 'Birth'. I caught a warm smile from Eluned Morgan, third row, in the congregation. Afterwards our women politicians, Jane Hutt, Elin Jones, Leanne Wood were outside, and we exchanged warm hugs. In the vestry I shook hands with Charles, and our Assembly Members.

*

News: twelve lovely boys, a young football team, and their coach, were freed from a flooded cave in Thailand. The very thought of it had kept me sleepless with nightmares of claustrophobia. At the news I feel my lungs fill with sweet air.

And next year Faber will publish my *Gododdin*.

12 July

The wren is singing its heart out. Even better, yesterday our hare returned, longer, leaner, more golden, red, hot, alive on the lawn. It paused, then loped elegantly over the grass and down through the gap. Its presence salves the heart-wounding ugliness of politics: in Britain, in America, and across Europe. Years ago I remember how David's anxiety about work was lifted by watching a pair of fox cubs playing in the larch wood, and, another time, another worry was washed away by dolphins leaping in the sea just off the prom in Aberystwyth. Such sweet natural events, together with 'Us', human closeness, must get us through these ugly times.

Sunday, 15 July

We expected Phil Thomas and Michael, visiting from Yorkshire, for lunch. After breakfast the phone rang. I heard David say: 'Stay there, walk to the prom, have a coffee at Gwesty Cymru, and I will come and get you.' The brakes went on their car last night, and they were stuck in Aberystwyth. They found the only garage in Ceredigion open on Sunday, and the car would be fixed tomorrow. I got lunch ready, a big bowl of warmed chicken salad, and summer pudding. They reached Blaen Cwrt at two. We sipped, ate, talked, and all was convivial. Phil is brilliantly entertaining, and he talks and talks, while lovely Michael quietly notices I might need help, and comes to assist. He is creating a beautiful knot garden at their newly acquired grand house, Knedlington Old Hall. He and David had much architectural and restoration matters to discuss, and supper time came, so I made mushroom and prawn risotto, with cheeses and grapes for afters. At ten David drove them to their B&B in Lledrod. He got back at midnight.

Glad to be cool. Glad to sleep.

25 July

I had a full house for my lecture on Dylan Thomas in Manchester. I did not know what to expect, but it was such a relief to see all the people. I enjoyed myself, let my love of Dylan's poetry lead me astray, and I went way off-script. I was a little worried that my 'talk' took off, leaving the printed 'lecture' behind, as quotes from Dylan's prose and poetry occurred to me. It was Carol Ann's first 'People's Lecture', as she calls the series, and to my relief she was pleased. She said it 'set the bar' for others. I was happy. I did not know I could give 'a lecture', or that it would be well received.

30 July

I have been reading the *Mabinogi*, and have been through my version of *Gododdin*, slowly reading aloud, listening, making adjustments. All translations by others are here on the table while I try to work out what I am doing, what I ought to do, and how to explain it in a preface. I think of it day and night.

July 2019

2 July

We sat on the terrace this evening listening to a whispering tribe of long-tailed tits in the trees, close to us, in the hedge of beech and laburnum. They made such a fuss, fluttering and twittering as the young were fed tiny green grubs by the adult birds. There must have been thirty or more little birds and their parents, and they did not seem to mind which adult fed which fledgeling. They are a collective, kith and kin, a beautiful civilisation that set us thinking, talking, wishing, as ugly politics prevail on both sides of the Atlantic.

*

Hare lopes over the lawn and the terrace, right to left, south to north this time. This garden belongs to the hare. David has left swathes of grass uncut for it to shape its form, for insects to breed. He reports a garden tiger moth in the hedge by the vegetable beds. I learn it is a moth particularly local to this place, to south-west Wales, relishing the damp rushy soil of Cae Blaen Cwrt.

*

July: *Gorffenaf*
Summer's end. (*gorffen*: end. *haf*: summer.)

Every year I regret the moment when my blackbird stops singing, when his young are fledged and he has nothing to sing about, no more to do, no mate to attend, no nest, no nestlings to guard with song. His favourite spire used to be the summit of the ash tree, until it was lost to ash disease. This year he sang all day long from somewhere deep in the beech trees from early spring. Now we see him and his mate feeding their fledgeling young on the lawn, but his aria is over until next spring. It is difficult to get used to his silence. I hear it as an absence.

*

5–6 July

Up early and on the road by 7.30am, for the RSAW[1] conference in Portmeirion. I attended the whole day, and it gave me much to think about, to look at, to share, to hear good people like Sunand Prasad, and others. At the end of the day's programme we checked into our beautiful room in the Castle, to cool off, to wash, to lie close to an open window for an hour before dinner and good talk with our friends in architecture. I discovered that I share a birthday with Alan Francis, and I told him we both shared it with Frank Lloyd Wright. Next year we must celebrate. Home on Saturday morning.

7 July

Off again to Anna Dreda's festival, 'Poetry in the Barn' at Aardvark Books, Bucknell, Herefordshire, a hamlet on the Welsh border. A blackbird was still singing somewhere close by, seven days into July. Paul Henry and Jonathan Edwards were among the performers. Anna had created a splendid event in Aardvark's book barn, readings in the lofty space open to the yard, books beyond, a refreshment tent close by.

Home again. A long, long drive. Sleep, sleep, sleep.

10 July

Rain. Soft summer rain, and our blackbird silent on the lawn. The thrush sings, his throat slaked with rain, hidden somewhere in the trees. Such a song was never heard at Blaen Cwrt in the old days, before we leafed every space, replanting

1 Royal Society of Architects, Wales.

border hedges, replacing post-and-wire fencing with native trees, and planted our hornbeam avenue, greening the land, at almost a thousand feet high.

*

A few months ago Henbant offered to sell us the patch of land between the back wall of Blaen Cwrt and the road. Too narrow for their machines, it is just the western corner of their big field, which they recently bought from the man who farms the bleak, bare fields across the road behind us. The border bank and high hedge kept our back wall perpetually dark and damp. Once the field corner was ours, we had the bank removed. As Leonard Cohen sang:

'There is a crack in everything. That's how the light gets in.'

It is just a small scrap of field, but now Blaen Cwrt, no longer backed into the hill, basks, settled in a newly generous space. The house has light and air. I can almost hear it breathe. The new back garden's western border runs along the lane, the high bank along the road concealing us from view by all but the cabs of the tallest tractors. To the south a new hedge-bank planted with hazel separates our piece from Henbant's field. Sunlight floods the terrace from south and west, the back house wall is drying out, and when we step up into the new patch and look south over Henbant's field, the glorious view is unbroken as far as Llanllwni mountain's long blue silhouette. It is gorgeous.

*

There were once three beech trees on the garden border, beyond the terrace wall. I could see them from here at the table where I work, their foliage filling the glazed gable wall with 'beechen green'. They were planted as hedge-trees at least a century ago, I suppose, to mark Blaen Cwrt from the fields, but by the time we came here the unclipped hedge had grown into great trees. The largest, most magnificent of the trees rises from the bank to the east. The children's long-outgrown rope swing still hangs from its wide-spreading, lowest branches, which in places dip low enough to tangle with the long grass below – grass left uncut for the hare, for wild flowers and insects. The second tree stands where the bank turns the corner to extend an arm around the terrace. The branches of the two great trees reach into and mingle with each other, as, no doubt, their roots do too, communicating deep underground in the friendship of trees. The third beech tree grew closest to the house on the west-facing bank, but it was never more than a neglected hedgeling which outgrew its purpose. It leaned, shapeless, over our terrace and the low wall semicircling my wall garden – 'my' garden because it is I who plant it with rock plants, pull out encroaching grass, and let the wild things grow among the tame. Wall garden, terrace, house-end and garden were overshadowed by the hedgeling's shapeless inclination. It had to go. The remaining pair of mature beech trees, their graceful branches lifting and falling over the long grass beyond the low terrace wall, are all the better for the opened space and light around them.

To fell a tree is no easy decision. Our three beech trees leafed in sequence. The doomed beech, though shapeless and light-thieving, was always first to come into leaf. Second is the beech that marks the garden corner. In spring its branches, extending far over the grass, stir in the least breeze, its new leaves a delicious green, translucent with sunlight. In high summer its branches dip and rise when there seems to be no wind at all. It was always a fine tree, wider and taller than the hedgeling, now free to extend in newly opened space, catching the wind and flocks of passing birds. Today, last to come into leaf as always, the largest beech stands motionless, a green room for shade-loving plants and woodland things, its fingers reaching further every year. It's a tree for climbing and swinging, though the children have grown and gone. It is the most cautious of the beech trees to open in spring, though it is bigger, taller, its branches more wide-spreading, reaching far over the grass of what we call 'the Middle Lawn', on the far side of the bank. 'The Lawn' is here before me, between the house and the laburnum hedge, the 'Lower Lawn' far down beyond the vegetable beds and the polytunnel. Too much grass to mow!

I read that a beech tree drinks about fifty gallons of water a day. I listen, certain I can hear the suck, sip and swallow of trees drawing water from the deep earth. That all three trees had different times and habits of leafing and of losing their leaves in autumn proves that they are not related. They were probably planted as a hedgerow early in the last century, each tree with a different genetic source, unlike the elms of Britain all of which, it is believed, took their origin from a single tree brought by the Romans. When one elm became diseased, gradually every single elm in Britain succumbed and died.

*

From spring to late summer, few pleasures exceed sitting on the terrace sipping something cool, maybe:

> Cool'd a long age in the deep-delved earth,
> Tasting of Flora and the country green

and gazing into the arching green shade of those trees, moments I dream of in the long dark days of winter. I look up from my work now to see them through wide-open glass doors. Among the first trees to come into leaf, and usually late to turn and fall, they are a spring- and summer-long pleasure, and again beautiful as the leaves bronze in autumn. This beautiful summer, after our day's work on page or screen, and about the house and garden, it is good to sit out on the terrace to talk, sip, gaze into our closest beech tree and, beyond its branches, to the view over the fields, the lovely perspectives of close and far, our trees against the distant mountain.

However, this year it hurts: the cool green of leaves, the tender 'beechen green' has been destroyed by two freak weather events. The first was the heatwave in February, which urged the trees into leaf too early. The second freak weather event was in May, when an ice-wind blew in from the north. Since that day the foliage on the west side of the two old beech trees, *fagus sylvatica,* especially the one closest to where we sit on summer evenings – the one whose green canopy over the grass I have always loved gazing into at this time of year – is shrivelled and dead. Having leafed too soon in the wave of unseasonal February heat, every young leaf was burnt by the breath of winter in May.

The two beech trees are alive, but their foliage has not recovered. Every west-facing leaf, from top to bottom, is burnt. And so too is the beech-brake a field away at the end of Cae Blaen Cwrt, every tree wind-scorched and shrivelled. Soon we notice damaged beech trees throughout Ceredigion. We have not seen this before, though it is not the first time, as Shakespeare warns us: 'rough winds do shake the darling buds of May'.

But such things are happening more often now. The seasons are changing, and there is no escaping the fact that we are to blame. It is climate change which caused the unseasonal February heatwave, and then the icy blast in May, harming not only our trees, but thousands of beech trees throughout Ceredigion and beyond, as we see if we drive further afield. Our acer was damaged too, soon scattering brown leaves on the lawn. Despite the acer showing some signs of recovery, some regreening of lower branches, on our two great beech trees the leaves are shrivelled on every twig. July, and the trees look dead. No beechen green. No autumn gold to come this year. It hurts.

26 July

In June we think warm days will never end, but as July arrives, and the blackbird falls silent, something in the year turns. This year, all 'beechen green' destroyed, the Welsh word for July, *Gorffenaf*, is appropriate. There is consolation for the blackbird's silence in the voice of the thrush. There was a time, when the land was treeless, before we restored the hedges, planted the hornbeam avenue and many other trees, when the song thrush never sang here in the garden, nine hundred feet above sea level. Now the thrush is here every day. It sang for an hour this morning, took a rest, and returned to sing so close that it seems to be just outside the room. I gaze into the trees, but I can't see where he hides. Unlike Browning's thrush, ours does not 'sing each song twice over', but more often *thrice* over, before changing the refrain and singing that thrice over too. The thrush must be trilingual. It sings in Welsh, English and Latin.

*

On the way along the lane in the pick-up, we turn through the gate onto our land, and park at the edge of the oak wood, high above the bog, Rhos Llawr Cwrt, to watch a hare running the land. This year has been a good one for hares. The young hare which made a form in our garden last year returned every day until winter. In March two hares chased each other across the garden and into Cae Blaen Cwrt. Was 'our' hare one of them?

From our side of the lane the land rises steeply to the track at the edge of the oak wood and, above the track, oak trees clothe the slope all the way to the top; to the south, our neighbour's land falls and levels towards the fields along the Glowan valley, and the bogland of Rhos Llawr Cwrt. The lane is not really a direct way to anywhere, just a quiet route for walker or cyclist, or a slow car with windows wound down, its driver taking in the pure pleasure of it. 'Shadows numberless'.

At the end of the oak wood, a hedge-bank marks our farthest border. At the foot of the slope below the wood, along the lane that winds along the Glowan valley, a few ash trees survive, but they look diminished. The lane is a green arcade of oak, hazel, sycamore, rowan, hawthorn, blackthorn and ash, branches meeting overhead. Along the lane, the banks flower in a succession of bluebells, stitchwort, campion, violets, Jack-by-the-hedge, then foaming umbellifers, meadowsweet, cow parsley. A place for a car to slow, windows wound down, and just breathe.

July 2020

July. *Gorffenaf*: in Welsh tradition the last month of summer, and the chorale is over. The birds sang dawn until dark from spring into early summer. During the May heatwave we took tea to the bottom of the garden every afternoon to sip and listen to their oratorio. Birdsong is the sound of possession, the male's grand aria, 'these are mine, mine, mine', holding his small tract of land and sky, his mate, their nest, their eggs, the young. At the end of June, their work done, they fall silent but for twittering. Their fledgelings flown, the concert's over. Silence, but for the squeal of a woodpecker, click of a nuthatch, a chirrup of tits and finches. The blackbird's aria cut to a phrase.

*

It is healing to watch our four and a half thousand young trees in full leaf throughout their second summer, our twenty-year-old hornbeam avenue casting parallel shadows on the grass, the sheltering arms of restored hedges about the fields, and all the other trees we have planted. This year there is time to stand and stare, to watch trees grow, a leaf unfurling. I love our old trees – the beeches, chestnuts, sycamores all far older than I am, and they will long outlive me – and still a few surviving ash trees among their sick relations, and the stumps of the fallen.

Butterflies and Reindeer
August 2018

The hare has come home, bounding into the garden through the gap in the hedge. It goes where it wills. If it is the same hare, it has grown since its presence last year. Chased from its form in Henbant's field when the mower cut and turned the grass, it ran into the garden using its old route over the terrace, ate a flower, then loped onto the stretch of stony earth behind Blaen Cwrt. It returned in the evening to nibble the long grass by the fence, as we sipped in the sunshine in the setting sun. A hare-in-residence once more this year. Hare to stay!

The Presence

A small wind winds through rush and sedge,
movement, heartbeat halts at the edge
of the lawn, stillness of hinged limbs
under the oak's November flame.

Something powers the morning, stops the air,
holds me in the planet of its stare,
its silence, not gunshot and the scream
I heard once, waking from a dark dream

in another place, but a pulsing presence
red-brown beneath the trees, a sense
that such a living thing once seen
in that sunlit space will never be gone,

its breath a mist on the air
between field and lawn. There. Not there.

The great ash tree that grew in the bank beside the lane, which I could see from the table where I write every day, was the blackbird's singing spire. One of spring's most delicious moments was always the first note of that powerful song, ringing out from the tiny black silhouette at the top of the tree, before a single, silver, fronded leaf had opened.

Ash trees are doomed. Edward Thomas writes of imagining that he hears a girl's voice singing the Welsh song, *Llwyn On* (The Ash Grove), and feels 'a ghostly gladness', listening as he wanders in a grove of ash trees:

> With a ghostly gladness, as if I heard a girl sing
> The song of the Ash Grove soft as love uncrossed

Gerard Manley Hopkins heard the tree itself whispering with milky sighs.

One sad day, two years ago, our ash tree had to go. It grew between the garden and the drive, close to a great sycamore tree. Its loss was hard to bear. We had the sycamore felled to make space to build the studio, but we didn't miss it. Its absence set the sky and the ground free of its heavy shadow and its pock-marked leaves, and there are sycamores elsewhere in the garden and about the fields. There are other ash trees too, but they are all in trouble. One, further along the hedge that borders our land from the lane, is now a skeleton tree in a shroud of ivy. Another grows closer, in the hedge between the garden and the field, but its foliage is sparser every year. Other ash trees, among several sycamores, oaks and beeches, border the lane winding through the Glowan valley at the far end of our land. We watch them nervously for signs of sickness.

We'd hoped that the felling of the sycamore in the garden would let air and sunlight heal the ash tree, allowing it room to spread, to let fall its lacy shadows on the grass, the drive, and our little studio building in its shade. The lace-shadow of its fine leaves and stems draped the roof and walls of the studio. The blackbird sang from its spire all spring and summer until his nestlings had flown, and he had no further need to sing.

The ash was almost always the last tree to come into leaf, though not every year, as the rhyming long-term weather forecast warns:

Ash before oak, a summer soak.
Oak before ash, a summer splash.

We knew nothing, then, of *Chalara fraxinea* – ash dieback – or the ash borer beetle, until a tree surgeon called by a few years ago. He and his team were working for the council, checking on the height and spread of trees growing close to electric cables. The tree surgeon warned us that our ash was sick, but I did not want to believe him. We agreed to having the dead upper branches lopped, and hoped it might recover. The tree man shook his head doubtfully. He was proved right. The dead branches were removed, but time did not heal the tree. Disease moved into lower branches, and in the end we called in our neighbour, Rob, the woodland man, who felled the tree for us. Its trunk and branches lay piled at the far end of Cae Blaen Cwrt, our closest field, waiting to be sorted into sizes and stored for woodworking, or burning. We do not know how old our ash was, but a healthy ash tree can live for four hundred years. Since its felling, our sky is empty of its grace and the delicate symmetry of its leaves in summer, and the blackbird has lost his pulpit.

An ash tree is home to many birds and insects. Late to leaf and early to fall, the airy canopy lets sunlight into wild corners of a garden or a woodland floor, speckled shade for violets and wild garlic. It is home to the rare high brown fritillary butterfly, which I had lived in hope of seeing somewhere in the ashy borders of our land. Bullfinches feed on the winged seeds, and woodpeckers, owls, redstarts and nuthatches nest in ash trees.

*

Last year we noticed bare upper branches in some of the ash trees in the lane along the Glowan valley, and there are more this year. The trees along the lane, which arch over it forming a green roof, are mainly oaks, with hawthorn, hazel and rowan in between. We drive the lane slowly, noting every tree. There are some leafy fronds on the ash, and bare twigs against the sky. However, the latest news from the Woodland Trust is that they are all doomed. When they die other saplings will seed themselves to replace them, to knit the gaps and repair the tree tunnel, to let its shadows fall over the lane, to mark our border, housing birds and feeding insects, just as in our garden two chestnuts have spread their arms and grown into the space and newly generous air set free from the lost ash. But no tree can replace the ash tree's lacy profile against the sky, its shadow on the ground. When we lose them, what species of tree will move into the hedge to shade the lane below the wood? Sessile oak, maybe? But not, as the poet Gerard Manley Hopkins describes them, 'a tree whose boughs break in the sky'.

Ash Boughs

Not of all my eyes see, wandering on the world,
Is anything a milk to the mind so, so sighs deep
Poetry to it, as a tree whose boughs break in the sky.
Say it is ashboughs: whether on a December day and furled
Fast or they in clammyish lashtender combs creep
Apart wide and new-nestle at heaven most high.
They touch heaven, tabour on it; how their talons sweep
The smouldering enormous winter welkin! May

Mells blue and snow white through them, a fringe and fray
Of greenery: it is old earth's groping towards the steep
Heaven whom she childs us by.

4 August 2019

Home from Cumbria, a music festival in Kendal, a five-hour drive away. Apart from the M6, every road is bordered with flowers, rosebay willowherb, meadowsweet, cow parsley, hogweed, hemlock, and all along the way are rowan trees lit with scarlet berries. I imagine our rowan saplings reaching their young roots down into our few acres, hung with future fruit.

The festival raised a good crowd in the hall in Blackwell, the beautiful Arts and Crafts house by Baillie Scott at Bowness-on-Windermere. We arrived in time to see the house, and I found corners to sit and write my journal, one in the hall where my reading would be staged, then a window seat in the white drawing room, looking up from my journal to watch sunlight pass over the lake and the mountains.

I read poems with music and architectural connections, but began with 'Miracle on St David's Day', for Wordsworth. Then 'Sounding', for Leonardo, and for *I Fagiolini* who perform tomorrow. The room was full – including the poet, Kim Moore, with her husband and six-week-old baby – the audience was warm, and filled with generous book-buyers. Afterwards we met Martin Kemp, expert on Leonardo and Renaissance art, for supper in a restaurant in Kendal. The evening ended our month without alcohol, a glass of wine the more appreciated for the abstinence, and it was good to talk to Martin. The following evening, at St George's Church in Kendal, we heard *I Fagiolini*'s concert celebrating the fifth centenary of Leonardo's death. The concert was sold out, each part introduced by Martin. Ten singers, voices sounding the height, width, depth of the building with pieces by Tallis, Herbert Howells, Monteverdi, Bach, Josquin des Prez, Janequin, Daniel-Lesur. Last, they sang my poem 'Sounding', the earlier version titled 'Listen', written for composer Adrian Williams. It was beautiful to hear it.

After a visit to the Boat House, a newly designed boat museum, and lunch by the water, we drove to Grasmere, travelling the whole way through a tunnel of trees. Many are great beeches, much taller than ours, flourishing in the deeper Lakeland soil and without our altitude. Many roads were lined by ash trees, not yet showing signs of their deadly disease. Cumbria being scarcely above sea level, the hills look deceptively mountainous, and its milder climate offers trees an easier life.

*

Home in Ceredigion, I watch for butterflies, hoping for the arrival of painted ladies. I dislike the name, no doubt coined by a Victorian lepidopterist. I prefer *Vanessa cardui,* or its common name, the thistle butterfly. Ten years ago, one August afternoon in 2009, we witnessed a wonder. Owain was visiting with our grandsons, and as we sat on the terrace we saw the closest beech tree quivering as if on fire. It was clothed, leafed by thousands of trembling wings, more and more butterflies flying in until the great tree was gold-robed in butterflies, from lower branches to crown. We didn't see the arrival but suddenly noticed the tree flickering, a passing migration flown two thousand miles from Africa. Ten years on there is news of another great migration on the way from North Africa. The butterflies follow the sun to travel with the turning earth, aloft on warm air as it moves north, the first insects reaching Britain in May and June. Thistles, on which they nest, breed and lay their eggs, provide their caterpillars' favourite food. In autumn some manage to return to Africa, but most are born to die here at summer's end. Ten years ago was a good butterfly year, and so is this year. Warm days, wild flowers, weeds, areas of grass left uncut, are what all butterflies need. A while ago I planted a garden variety of thistle in my wall bed – it is in flower. Our wild thistles escape the scythe, and we leave areas of long grass in the garden and the fields for the insects and the hare. I wait for the first butterfly, imagining the beech leafed with wings as it was that day ten years ago.

5 August

My late mother's birthday, and she sends me a gift. Three thistle butterflies fly over the terrace and settle to feed on a big thistle in full flower – *Eryngium bourgatii* – in my wall garden. At the time of the last migration, commissioned to write a poem with an African connection, to read in Westminster Abbey, I wrote 'A Wind from Africa':

> Was it reading the butterfly book in the garden,
> the common verse of the field,
> the lovely litany of *lepidoptera*?
> *Orange tip. Peacock. Meadow Brown. Red Admiral.*
> *Small Heath. Gatekeeper. Ringlet. Tortoiseshell.*
> *Brown Hairstreak. March Fritillary.*
>
> Was it a flick of the jetstream's tail, the must
> of lion breath, that southern wind that brings
> the swallows in a veil of Saharan dust,
> that made the beech tree suddenly sing
> with a thousand flickering flames
> the unheard whispering of wings?

It spun with dancers, too many, too quick,
a whirl of desert red and marigold,
amber, umber, Moroccan gold,
Vanessa cardui, born in the Atlas mountains,
wings on the wind for a thousand miles.
over seas and continents.

All summer they lingered, a blur of wings
feeding on nectar, honeydew, burdock,
clearing thistle from our fields.
They live to breed, be beautiful and die.
In winter, their ghosts in the butterfly tree
are white wings falling, falling from the sky.

Trees, birds, insects, all the wild things, are bigger than our politics. They cure me of gloom. 'They will go on as dynasties fall'.

6 August 2019

Toni Morrison has died, after, they say, a short illness. I remember her words when she won the Nobel Prize for Literature: 'We die. That may be the meaning of life. But we do language. That may be the measure of our lives.'

She was eighty-eight, a life-measure too short. In a way, great writers never die. Shakespeare lives. Keats lives. In Hay, in May 2014, David and I were asked by Peter Florence to accompany Toni, and others, to lunch. We were quite a party, a table for six: Toni, and, as I recall, A.S. Byatt, Carmen Callil, Ian McEwan, David and me. It was a happy party, rich with good talk, and there was one unforgettably funny moment. Toni was wearing a black jersey sweater. Puddings came. She had a baked peach. Talking, laughing, sipping, feasting, suddenly a portion of peach leapt from her spoon to begin travelling down her chest. We held our breath. Then her lower lip began to wobble, and she said in a child's voice: 'My peach wouldn't cut!' And we all laughed in joyous shared relief. Such a brilliant writer, such a lovely, funny woman, prepared to laugh at herself, and with us.

'We die. That may be the meaning of life.' I consider her words, determined to reread every word she wrote, but thinking too of the ash trees, and what the poets have to say about them.

8 August 2019

Storwm Awst. The August Storm. A rush of rain and a sudden wind in the trees. In Welsh, July is *Gorffenaf,* Summer's end. *Gorffen* – end. *Haf* – summer. I forget, while the sun warms the terrace, and we sit out sipping, as we did yesterday for our friends Mary and Richard's visit, and the mown grass smells sweet, and the garden needs watering, that the *storwm Awst* will come, because it always does. This year it comes earlier and wilder than ever. Trees are down, trains cancelled, power stations out and electricity cut. Here it is just wild and windy, darkening with brief, heavy downpours arriving without warning. The *Eisteddfod Genedlaethol*[1] has sent its young campers home, and set other safety measures. But Jim Parc Nest has won the Chair, for a second time, this time in his eighties. Happy news. We prepare for Catrin to visit for her house-sitting week, while we fly to Sweden for the Alpine Fellowship Symposium.

*

1 National Eisteddfod.

12 August

Catrin is here. This morning she saw the hare run from behind the house, across the terrace and the lawn and through the gap. We leave her and her dog as big as a horse, Raffi the Rhodesian ridgeback, to enjoy the place until Poli and their other dog arrive on Tuesday, by which time we will be in Fjällnäs in Sweden, for our symposium on 'Identity'. I am asked to read a poem after dinner at an art installation in the forest on the first evening, and to read in the dining hall on Saturday. I will be political!

*

13–18 August

We are in Sweden with the Alpine Fellowship, leaving Catrin in charge of Blaen Cwrt. We flew from Cardiff to Amsterdam, thence to Oslo, and with one more leap onward to Røros on a little toy plane, and finally a drive for an hour by taxi through birch forests, past lakes, with reindeer grazing by the road, across the Norwegian-Swedish border, where the blue and gold flag welcomes us back home into the European Union.

After so many hours and miles, we arrive at Fjälnäs. Far from any town, set among forests, lakes and surrounding hills, is a splendid golden timber hotel among its own chalets, barns, timber buildings, all painted in typical Scandinavian colours of pastel grey, yellow ochre, old Persian red.

We are welcomed, and led to our red-painted chalet. It is the loveliest space on the grassy shore of a lake, with views to the south and west. Close by, a herd of reindeer grazes, and rising fish make silver nose-ripples on the surface of the lake. Across the water, a forest rises, and distant mountains. All is light, space, water and trees.

I can hardly bear to leave our chalet, but thence to dinner, to meet Alan Lawson and Jacob – whose idea all this was in the first place – and our company of Alpine Fellows: Nell Leyshon whom we met in Venice two years ago, Jessica, theatre producer, the poet John Burnside, Damian Le Bas, a writer from the traveller community, Julian Spalding, critic, and his French wife, and so many others who would be part of our five days of rich, international, intercultural conversation and company, sharing delicious food, poetry, music, drama, debate.

*

After dinner I am charioted up the hill in the dark in a buggy bouncing up the mountain track through the forest, where an art installation awaits its moment. We few stand in the dark waiting for the walking Alpinists to arrive. It is pitch black but for the dance of approaching torches. I dare not move, the stony ground beneath my feet made the rougher by the many journeys of the artist, Lyall Sprong, and his assistants, who have been working for weeks to prepare their surprise. All are here.

Suddenly, in the darkening sky above the track ahead, over a gap in the forest trees, we see our earth, our planet, huge and luminous hanging in space. There is a great collective gasp, like a wind, almost, and someone begins quiet chanting in a languagefrom the south of African. Spiritual, beautiful, thrilling, standing in the pitch darkness, seeing our earth as if from space. I am holding a book in the dark. Someone switches a torch on, and I read. My poem for Leonardo da Vinci.

*

A wonderful week. Water. Reflections. Reindeer. Forests. Distant hills. Conversation. Good people from all parts of Europe and further afield were a small world. The final supper is the most delicious, delicate, elegant food I have ever eaten. The chef, brought in specially to cook our last meal, is Helena Puolakka, the famous chef from Finland, who had created a series of small courses made of local fare, fish, fowl and fungi from the fields, forests, rivers and lakes in the landscape around us.

Between dessert and coffee, my reading. It was warmly received, and connected me to people I had not spoken to before. Julian Spalding, with a smlle of pleasure, keeps quoting from my poem, *Llŷr*, 'Nothing is until it has a name.'

19 August

Home again. Wales too is beautiful. After wild wet weather the sun is on the fields, and we have three days to enjoy the bank holiday, the two of us, to sip on the terrace in the evening, have supper at the garden table. Sad, dead beech leaves drift onto the terrace and the lawn with every breeze, but we note the big, gold wings of a few remaining thistle butterflies, *Vanessa cardui,* wavering home to their roost.

Yesterday afternoon a tiny bat flew towards the house pursued by swallows, its wings beating hell for leather. I have never seen a bat in full sunlight before. It flew fast, straight, desperate, not circling for insects. By evening, while other bats were out scribbling the air, feeding on invisible insects, it had gone.

*

Bank Holiday Monday. A cloudless day. Against the sky's perfect blue the tiny bat is back, flying over the lawn pursued by swallows. Its wings seem to beat rapidly, but low and straight, slow enough for its body, face and ears to be clearly visible. It must be in trouble, ill, exhausted, confused, hungry, though we didn't see it swoop for insects. Henbant's tractor hisses over the field tossing the grass beyond the new border bank between us and them. Then silence. Heat. Grass dries in the sun. We lunch on the terrace.

Evening. Time slows for us to go over the day. We gaze, listen, allowing ourselves a gin and tonic today, and later a bottle of wine. Hours to sip and sup as the sun slips west, amazed at the garden we have made from the wilderness. It is no grand garden, just grass and trees, form, perspective, glimpses, gaps, views into small spaces, close and far vistas, the colour of shrubs, perennial plants. Blue, cream, and rose-red hydrangeas, orange crocosmias, spears of acanthus, a dazzle of daisies, all gradually planted over the years, and hoped for. In the end they have all found and filled their place and shape. And still a few butterflies, their large gold wings luminous and backlit by the sun, visit the big blue thistle on the wall garden.

These three late August days are good for David, a pause in the battle with all who hinder the achievement of architecture.

31 August 2019

August 2018 came in with the hare, and August 2019 is borne away by the hare. It runs the terrace, left to right, north to south, pauses, looks at me through the glass. Exits stage right. There. Not there.

1941. The Great Silence. I am four years old. There are no cars. Birds are singing. On the other side of the road is the park, where Cold Knap Lake is a mirror. On the far side of the lake, all along the seafront of Pebbly Beach, ugly concrete blocks and cruel, giant rolls of barbed wire line up. 'To stop the Nazis,' my father explains. Hitler has invaded Russia, but my father says he can't come here. I listen through the wall, hear voices on the radio, the words people say to each other over my head behind their hands. 'Hush! The child!' There is an enemy let loose on the world, and danger everywhere. In the park, on Pebbly Beach, in the Little Harbour, in Porthkerry woods, in the cupboard under the stairs where I'm put down to sleep with my bear if there is shouting in the sky. A monster is on the run, and I make a picture of it. I look at the names of places in the lit cave of the radio: Paris, Brussels. Berlin. Sometimes the radio says their name. I turn the knob. I say them. It's called geography. I can read. I watch my mother's finger touch the words as she reads me stories, so I know what their shapes say.

August 2020

The Great Silence. I have not left our house, the garden and land, since returning from Cardiff on 10 March, the day after a reception for Cymru'n Cofio – Wales Remembers – where we gathered in the Senedd to note the ending of the First World War. I read my commissioned poem for the occasion: 'Was it for This?', its theme, 'holy glimmers of goodbyes', words Wilfred Owen left singing in our minds.

There is a new vocabulary: self-isolation, furlough, lockdown, shielding for the old and the vulnerable. It is unprecedented in my lifetime: theatres, pubs, shops, offices all closed, cities and towns silent, empty, and people under order to stay home. All my readings, gigs, workshops, lectures are cancelled, all festivals, Poetry Live events, theatres, and the fees that come with them. Yet I am happy to be here, to go nowhere, to stay home, eat our own vegetables, find forgotten food deep in the freezer, to make cawl, bread, Welsh cakes, to cook, to forage. We relish the silence, the empty roads and clean, clear skies. Every dawn is the earth's first morning. It is not the first time. Plagues have come before, and the world has continued.

Lockdown. We have worked at home for months, writing, making architecture, at either ends of the dining table, and, in David's case, gardening a few hours a day, or out with his tools making something, building something. I look up from my work through two glazed walls, long views to east and south over the garden and fields to the horizon. Before me the sun rises over the trees, sails to high noon through the glazed south gable wall, and lays its last light on the terrace as it sets behind the house. Day after day, these months, March to October on our high hill, we've watched the slow transition from bare winter branches to summer luxuriance, seen first leaves opening, foliage burgeoning across Blaen Cwrt's green acres, now loosening gold. Once a poor smallholding in bleak, treeless hillcountry, now it is deep in trees, all distance lost in foliage. To see the horizon we must pass the two great beech trees to the Middle Lawn, or step up onto the terrace. Today, to the east through the hedge-gap, past the oak dipping its boughs at the fenced edge of the field, Gethin's sheep graze close to the fence. Animal, innocent, they lie in the sun, nibbling.

I don't feel isolated. Creatures share our land, our woods and fields, our sky, our garden. The hare, a young fox, a clutch of rabbits. Enemies come too – rats, and those alien tree rats, grey squirrels. Our favourite is the hare, cwtched in its form at the edge of the lawn, nibbling a stem before lying stone still for hours, then coming and going as it will. A few months ago the young fox lay asleep in the evening sun on the bank at the edge of Cae Blaen Cwrt – the home field. When it woke, we heard it calling, hungry, alone. No vixen came to its rescue, so it left its grassy lair and came into the garden, crossed the terrace and dipped its head to drink from the moat that borders the glass wall of this room. It could not reach the water, so I filled a bowl and offered it. It returned at dusk. We watched it lapping like a dog in the twilight.

Spending so much time together, 'self-isolated' in acres of grassy space, gave rise to a need for the 'naming of parts'. We created the garden, about a third of an acre that extends a few hundred yards to the border of a neighbour's land, by stealing a length from the home field, Cae Blaen Cwrt. The three lawns lie before me, one just below the terrace, one beyond the hedge that once divided the farmyard from the fields, and one down at the end of the garden, on our eastern border. Linked by grass paths, they need names to distinguish one from the other: 'Where will you be? Where shall I bring the tea?' Closest is The Lawn, once the old farmyard, long overgrown by grass and nettles when I first saw it forty five years ago. A scythe, and later a lawnmower tamed it. On the far side of the hedge, glimpsed from my workplace through gaps in the laburnums, is the Middle Lawn. Way down at the end of the garden, past the raised vegetable beds, the blueberry patch and the polytunnel, is the Orchard Lawn – grand name earned by three apple trees, a plum tree and a quince. It is sheltered by a grove of white-stemmed birches, clipped beech hedges, and, on the border, copper beech, oaks, chestnut and sycamore. Behind the house the newest 'lawn' is bathed in the last light of evening. Once a corner of our neighbour's big field, and reached up a steep, short slope from the rear house wall, we call it the Back Lawn. For months it has been a sea of unmown long grasses, flowers, seed heads and insects, a shimmering sight in the low evening sun, a small wild meadow, mowed in August, once grasses had seeded, and butterflies have done with it.

In late August, the *storwm Awst* brought a rage of Atlantic hurricanes, tantrums of wind and rain, one after another, ripping summer to rags.

The Angelus Tree
September 2018–19

Every September I think about elm trees. They were the first trees I loved, two elms in particular. On a September morning long ago, a single, repeated bell-note woke me from a bad dream in which I was lost in a wood. At the end of every track I had to make a choice between two paths. Which one should I choose? Which would lead me out of green darkness into a sunlit field, and the familiar way home?

I was eleven years old, waking in a strange room. A dormitory. A word from stories. The bell that woke me sounded close by. Outside the window, at the western, right-hand edge of a lawn mowed into neat stripes, stood three great trees. I would learn that they were elms. They touched the sky with their quivering, cloudy crowns, and I imagined they had been there forever and ever. Between the two tallest elms a plank was nailed, and from it hung a bell and a long rope. Swinging rhythmically on the bell-rope with all her strength was a young nun. Her feet left the ground with every pull. She was ringing the Angelus – Latin for angel – a call to prayer I would hear twice a day in term time for the next seven years. I think she was having fun, swinging, ringing, flying through the air.

A new girl, the first pupil to arrive for the start of the autumn term, I had spent the night alone and lonely in the six-bed dormitory that overlooked the lawn. 'Our Lady's dorm', we would call it. All rooms bore the names of saints and holy ones. Each bed was neatly tucked in with what I would learn to call 'hospital corners', and covered with a slippery gold counterpane.

I don't know why I had arrived a day early. I remember a nervous tea with my mother and father at the Seabank Hotel, Porthcawl, before they drove me the few miles to the village of Newton, to the convent school established in an old house that stood high on a rock above the village and the road that ran through sand dunes to the sea. The dormitory window looked across the lawn, and the yet-to-be-discovered secret garden, which was reached through a gate, down steep steps cut in the rock. Later I would learn it was where nuns went to pray privately, to meditate, to murmur the rosary, to be alone and sometimes, as I recall, to cry. Beyond the lawn stretched the sand dunes, and beyond them shone the sea that surged over and against Tusker Rock, with its stories of shipwreck and pirates, then the islands of Flat Holm, Steep Holm, and the far blue shadow of England.

Ours was not a Catholic or even a particularly religious family. I was from chapel-going people on my father's side, and my mother's family were Church in Wales. I had passed the scholarship and won a place at Penarth Grammar School, but my mother decided I should go to a boarding school in Porthcawl, thirty miles from home. I was troubled and troublesome. My parents' marriage was unhappy, and I knew it. Money was short. My mother was busy running our home as a guest house. She was anxious for the family to 'go up in the world'. The convent boarding school, St Clare's, was recommended by well-off friends. I was a bookworm, addicted to reading anything in print, but especially Penarth public library's shelves of Enid Blyton's Malory Towers stories, with their prospect of midnight feasts in the dorm and daring rescues from burning buildings. Boarding school, instead of helping my mother make beds and do the washing-up. I needed no persuading.

Across a lifetime and that remembered lawn, those cloud-headed elms and their tolling bell sing and sound my memory. There were other elms in the convent garden. By the time I reached the sixth form I was lodged with three elderly sisters in their cottage next to the school. It stood by a bend in the road at the foot of the rock on which the convent stood, and was reached down a flight of steps cut in the rockface. Beside the gate, through which I passed night and morning on the path between the school building and my room, there stood another great elm. I stroked it in passing, touched the silvery map of its bark, and its silk leaves opening low on the trunk. The elm that watched me safe home every night, and the Angelus trees, became so familiar they were like friends. Every spring, lines of Browning came to mind, and again now as I remember:

> The lowest boughs and the brushwood sheaf
> Round the elm-tree bole are in tiny leaf[1]

Studying Art and Art History for A level, (as well as English and French), I discovered Constable's paintings of trees. His work excited me into trying to draw and paint my elms. He made me look closer, and to notice an elm wherever it grew, most often a solitary tree, a dreamer at the border of a field, narrow at the bole, its lofty head a green cloud in the sky.

September 2019
Thursday 5 September

We drive to Newport to park the car at Mary and Richard's house, and Richard drives us to Bristol airport for our flight to Italy. Once freed from the horror of the airport, the flight is swift and smooth, and soon we are driving south in the hired car to San Gimignano, a beautiful medieval walled town in Siena. We walk from the car, uphill through the gate in the wall and the narrow cobbled street to Hotel Bel Soggiorno,

---

1 'Home-Thoughts from Abroad', Robert Browning.

find our room with its balcony overlooking the street, leave our luggage and wander off, David and I and Richard and Mary, for dinner on a lovely terrace overlooking a valley so deep and hidden in trees that I think its wooded slopes must conceal a river. But down below is just the town. It is good to talk and dine together, and at last, after a long, long day, a relief to sleep in our room overlooking the alley, the buildings, the golden stone of medieval Italy.

Friday 6 September

We set off for Sant' Antonio, Tivoli, a Renaissance monastery associated with the poet Horace, restored by the Landmark Trust. We unpack, wander, settle. I soon discover nooks and sheltered places within the house and the garden to write. One storey down below the house, level with its basement and reached by a flight of rough stone stairs, is a grove of ancient olive trees. Across the valley a waterfall drops from a great height. Falling water. A glory of shining sound. We learn that it is not a natural waterfall, but a section of the river diverted to prevent flooding in the town. The fall is switched on in the morning and off at night. I make sure I don't miss the moment, watching from our bedroom window to see and hear it begin, and fall still and silent at night.

*

I am in the loggia, Sant' Antonio, Tivoli, Italy, with my journal, notebooks, pen and iPad. It is the perfect writing space, shady, with warm winds that rise like breathing from deep in the valley. Across the green, forested gulf is the waterfall, the town on the hill, and blue dissolving distances that lead to Rome. The gardener is mowing. David, and our architect friends, known, including us, as the Perfect Ten – Mary, Richard, Helen, Alan, Chris, Jacqui, Bella, Lyndon – are exploring.

I intend to spend my time here looking, listening, writing, strolling the garden of gnarled old olive trees and fruit trees. We all go our own way. By day I make myself a space, sometimes in the cool shade of the loggia, sometimes on a little verandah that looks over the valley and miles of rural Italy receding and fading to far blue hills, or on a shady seat in the garden, writing, listening, relishing. David, and the others, sketch, add a piece or two to a giant crossword, wander, trek, swim, come and go. Every evening, after a glass in the cloister, we gather in the great dining room for dinner cooked by lovely Maria.

And so the days pass, with visits to Tivoli, the glorious gardens of Villa d'Este, and once to a lofty terrace restaurant for a fine dinner with all of Lazio spread before us. I think about the poet Horace, who loved and frequented this place, and haunts it still. The ancient and gnarled descendants of his olive trees shade the garden, his poetry sings, and the cool space of the ancient basement room where they dry the lavender holds ancient voices.

After eight beautiful days, we drive to Pienza, for lunch at a restaurant overlooking infinity, which Beckett said was the best view in Italy. Thence to Montepulciano, the Meublé Il Riccio, rooms in a building of staircases, halls and inner courtyards off the square, again with a view of forever and ever. Then, at last, we drive to Pisa airport, to Bristol, and home.

Postscript, September 2019

Every morning from the bathroom window I note with horror tree rats – grey squirrels – scuttling through the hazel, nut-gathering for winter. I wish them gone. They are alien beasts, the enemies of young trees and nesting birds. They steal birds' eggs. They have driven away the native red squirrel we used to see here years ago. They are damaging trees in our hornbeam avenue, biting a ring of bark all round the young trunk to suck the sap from the sweet green under-layer, cutting off the supply of sap to the branches. It is estimated that grey squirrels kill one in twelve trees in a plantation over fifteen years old, when the trees are strong enough to support their weight, the bark not yet tough enough to resist their teeth. Of our twenty-four hornbeams, planted in December at the turn of the millennium, one has died, one is dying, others are damaged. Grey squirrels attack trees between ten and forty years old, from April to July. Hateful beasts! In ten to twenty years' time will they attack our young woodland trees, now rising and spreading on the Fron?

September 2020

Blaen Cwrt has been without domestic animals for too long, allowing the wilderness in: mice in the house, eating their way through clothes, a rattle of grey squirrels in the roof-space, rats in the garden. High time to bring cats to Blaen Cwrt once more. We contacted an animal rescue centre in Haverfordwest. They came to check, approved us, and recommended a pair of one-year-old tortoiseshell sisters. David collected them. We renamed them Mali and Medi. They settled quickly, nuzzled us, bonded, fed, slept, fought each other, used the litter tray neatly. But, being young, they were climbing on cupboards, leaping eight feet to the sill of the gable window. We risked letting them out after two days, instead of the recommended two weeks. It was worth it. They sniffed the air, stepped out, wandered and returned, knowing they live here now. They are wild animals, and they are domestic creatures. Wild and tame, they wander, hunt, kill, bring prey home, nuzzle us to connect and belong. Tree rats, and all vermin, have disappeared. Mali and Medi have dealt with the problem.

Another September

Trees, and architecture. Long ago when I was an undergraduate reading English in Cardiff University, my three years were made the more pleasurable by the walk which I made twice daily between town and the main college building, under the arching shade of the double row of elms that ran along King Edward VII Avenue, flanked by the white buildings of the Civic Centre. The elms' branches met overhead, their tracery of blue shadows falling on the rose-red road below. I had known them all my life, from Saturday visits with my father to the museum, or to his office at the BBC in Park Place. By the time I was ten years old, I was entranced by the Civic Centre, the white city. It is a remarkable piece of planned civic architecture, prompted by the first Marquess of Bute, who gave the fifty-eight acres of parkland to the city on condition that trees and green spaces were preserved and its new buildings designed by his chosen architects. I loved its enticing paths leading through lawns and trees, its white buildings made of Portland stone.

My favourite stone bear, couchant on Cardiff Castle wall with his fourteen fellow beasts, was the gatekeeper to the white city, its gardens and broad avenues of trees, its buildings with tall pillars, domes, a dragon, and a clock tower you could see from miles away. Inside the white palaces were marble halls, curving staircases, statues, patterned tiles, lofty spaces where I felt part of a fairy story. It was another country, and it was mine.

As a child, my reward for being good, while my father checked mail in his office, was our Saturday visit to the museum: across Park Place, past the Gorsedd Gardens, up the wide flight of steps, under the white-pillared portico, and into the soaring space of the hall. I ran to my favourite treasure: the stuffed fox, paw lifted, yet frozen forever in his glass case. A little later, it was the blue lady I most often visited, Renoir's *La Parisienne*, dressed in every blue in the world, lapis lazuli, cobalt, indigo, sky, the blue of Porthkerry bluebell woods. A recent visit to the gallery reminded me that I know that painting as I do, and others in the Davies sisters' bequest to the museum, because I grew up with them. As far as I was concerned, they were mine, or ours, as I believe the Davies sisters intended when they gifted their art collection to the city. Years later, a nervous new student at the Freshers' Ball, I knew that the City Hall was mine too, as I ran up the staircase into the Marble Hall, past statues of Welsh heroes, to dance to the music of John Dankworth and Cleo Lane.

The elm avenue was involved with the joy and the excitement of discovering the widening world of literature, especially poetry. A block of white stone. I used to touch one stone for luck every morning as I passed through the portal of the university into the dusk of the entrance hall. Leaves, falling in autumn as the term began. Words, first unfurlings in spring, damp with birth. Later, rising tension as exams brought anxiety, but also a strange excitement. Lying on the grass in summer revising, in the public gardens just over the road. As I walked out of the green cathedral of the elm avenue and crossed the park into the university, out of dazzling sunlight into the shade and lofty space of the main hall, I felt I was walking through history. Trees and stones were telling me the story of building. I imagined how early man, our ancestors, living in caves or in the ancient forest that covered this island, might have been inspired by trees to imagine pillared spaces made by placing stone on stone, and to raise overhead, a lofty branching roof. Words, stones, trees. Architecture is the poetry of stone, as, maybe, I imagined in my poem, 'Llandâf Cathedral':

> first mark, first word, first hymn to awe.
> first poem with something to say of the human heart,
> first vision of a building taller than the forest,
> aisled, vaulted, clerestoried with sunlight, imagined
> into being, because we were forest-dwellers once
> and learned our metaphors from trees.[1]

The power of public buildings and their arrangement have a profound influence on all who live and work among them. Buildings. Trees. We need beautiful spaces, and value and rejoice in 'commodity, firmness and delight'[2] in our urban surroundings: the street sweeper, a tramp asleep on a bench beside a statue, rough sleepers in their tents along the canal, the man who spears litter in the park, the men and women who arrive before dawn to clean a public building, the bin-lorry men at the back doors, students basking on the lawns outside the university, the museum's conservators, secretaries and doormen and chattering flocks of children herded by their teachers. All, who come from the terraced streets, estates and suburbs of the city where they live, on entering the designed unity of white buildings in a Civic Centre set among green

---

1 Landâf Cathedral, *A Recipe for Water*, 2009.

2 'Well building hath three conditions: firmness, commodity and delight', Vitruvius.

spaces, gardens and trees, can claim great buildings as their own for a few hours, inhabit them, and be inhabited by them, all their lives.

After the shops and traffic, across the canal where boys dived for pennies, something new began every day for me. Gardens. White stone. In its fifty-eight acres white buildings gleamed among the gardens in a perspective of luminous palaces leading through tree-lined avenues. The daily walk to college from Central Station took me up St Mary Street, High Street, past Greyfriars, over the canal, up the rose-red avenue of elms, through Alexandra Gardens, over Museum Place and through the white stone portal into the cool entrance hall of University College. I remember meeting my tutor to discuss my Spenser essay at a window seat in the half-light of the main hall; my Anglo-Saxon seminar in a little room up a narrow stone staircase, coal smoking in the grate; sitting summer exams every June as, in those long-ago days, the brass bands of the Miners' Gala Parade passed by. In the upstairs gallery of the college library, where I studied for those exams, were little 'rooms', a table, chairs, each space almost enclosed by a pair of bookcase 'walls', the third wall a book-lined walkway, the fourth open to a spacious view from the lofty ceiling to all that was happening on the floor below. I cannot forgive the much later barbaric destruction of that generous space, and its little rooms-with-a-view, by the insertion of a mezzanine floor. Nor do I forgive those who bulldozed the ruins of Greyfriars at the south end of the Civic Centre. I remember public outrage in the 1970s at a City Council transport department proposal to destroy the famous animal wall to make room for a highway and overpass. Public outrage saved the wall, and my favourite stone beast. The bear.

The double avenue of elms was planted for the third Marquess of Bute in 1779–80. My green cathedral. I walked that way – it was not the shortest route – in every season, when the elms were in full leaf just to see how the giants touched fingers across Edward VII Avenue, or in winter the way their shadows lay on snow. The map shows the fifty-eight acres of its architectural plan. At the far north end of Edward VII Avenue and Museum Avenue, Corbett Road draws a line west to east, a conclusion, the end. But it isn't, quite. On the north side of Corbett Road the design of the two avenues of trees and roads continues through Queen Anne Square, separating yet connecting white stone and red brick, the civic and the domestic. The border is marked by a white stone screen, through which we see the parallel lines of two tree-lined roads retreating into the green distance, running the length of a wide central lawn between the red-brick houses of the exclusive little estate. The screen and the square commissioned by the last Marquess of Bute were, my research revealed, designed by the architect, Howard Williams. Thus I have two family connections with the creation of Cardiff's Civic Centre, 'the white city built on black gold', the wealth produced by coal. My late father-in-law, and his father before him, were miners in Oakdale Colliery, part of the South Wales Coalfield which enriched the city and made Cardiff the biggest coal-exporting dock in the world; Howard Williams, last architect to be commissioned, by the last Marquess of Bute, to design Queen Anne Square and the screen at the north end of the Civic Centre, was my Uncle Howard.

One spring day in the 1970s, I drove down King Edward VII Avenue into town. No lacy shadows fell over the car as I moved with the traffic, crawling slowly down the rose-red road. The elm was brought to Britain by the Romans, and it is thought that all our elms were clones of a single tree. The lack of genetic diversity made them susceptible to infection. On the grass verges on either side lay all that was left of the elm avenue, felled two hundred years after their planting, dead from Dutch elm disease. Their cathedral majesty reduced to firewood.

Cardiff Elms

Until this summer
through the open roof of the car
their lace was light as rain
against the burning sun.
On a rose-coloured road
they laid their inks,
knew exactly, in the seed,
where in the sky they would reach
precise parameters.

Traffic-jammed under a square
of perfect blue I thirst
for their lake's fingering
shadow, trunk by trunk arching
a cloister between the parks
and pillars of a civic architecture,
older and taller than all of it.

Heat is a salt encrustation.
Walls square up to the sky
without the company of leaves
or the town life of birds.
At the roadside this enormous
firewood, elmwood, the start
of some terrible undoing.

Now the horse chestnut too is officially considered vulnerable to extinction, threatened by a particular moth, and disease. I watch our chestnuts nervously. There is too much undoing.

An Ash Root
October 2018

'October is marigold.' So Ted Hughes wrote, briefly and beautifully, on one long-ago October morning, when he found that a glass of wine left out in the garden overnight had formed a skin of ice, a premonition of another Ice Age. He did not foresee that the opposite would come about to threaten the earth. Heat. Rising temperatures. Flood, fire, famine.

This October there is no ice, no purifying bite of frost to turn leaves marigold before they fall, only unseasonably warm days and nights, wild Atlantic winds hurling torrential rain, the rags and remnants of transatlantic hurricanes. The wind swept all the beech leaves on our terrace into neat piles in corners against the walls, saving me a job. This October, we fear not another Ice Age but the loss of ice, and consequently rising seas threatening to drown low-lying countries, and to burn our planet.

Summer is over. The year is growing old. I remember, years ago, on holiday in France one sweet September, David and I visited the beautiful golden village of Saint-Amand-de-Coly, with its fortified church where the uneven floor slopes steeply up from the door to the altar. Outside the church we met an old woman, bent, scarved and robed in black. She greeted us courteously, and closed our short conversation by murmuring sadly, half to us, half to herself: '*l'été va vite maintenant*'. It was as if she were speaking not just of the summer, but the summer of her own life ebbing quickly away. That was years ago, when I thought I would never grow old. I am not sure that I have, yet!

*

From the 1970s, when we still had children to look after, and our working lives were in Cardiff, Blaen Cwrt was our refuge from the city, our summer house. I first saw it, a ruined *bwthyn*[1] in a wilderness of nettles, in 1974. It was owned at the time by Hywel and Nana Williams of Fron Felen farm, half a mile down the lane. They farmed the neighbouring fields on both sides of the lane that ran down to the little river Glowan.

Up the lane Blaen Cwrt, a smallholding in a state of ruin, was for sale. A single-storey longhouse, two rooms and a barn under one long roof, its overgrown yard and garden overwhelmed by grass and nettles. Sheep sheltered in its two rooms. An owl lived in its adjoining barn, birds nested in the chimneys. Unaware of current local planning regulations, that forbade the restoration of a house unoccupied for ten years (Blaen Cwrt had been empty for four decades), we spent every school holiday camping in the ruin, scything the nettles, fitting a front door, fixing the holes in the rusty roof and replacing the pair of small windows that flanked the central door with a replica pair, beautifully made by David's Uncle Bill.

Blaen Cwrt was soon made sound, left empty and alone in term time. Once, returning after a long winter absence, we found one of the little sash windows had been forced open, and the few small ornaments I had placed on the bar beside the catch had been removed and carefully set down on the window board. Someone – lovers? – seeking shelter, had removed one of the small panes of glass, unlatched the window, lowered the upper sash and eased through the narrow gap. I had done it myself once, when we forgot the key. Apart from one broken pane, they had done no harm, and were welcome to their hour of shelter.

Another time, our neighbour Hywel telephoned us in Cardiff to report something strange. One snowy morning,

1 cottage.

checking his sheep in the field on the other side of the lane, he noticed a track gouged through the snow, across the lane and under our gate. 'As if', he said, 'a pig had snouted its way through the snow.' But the snow-covered ground before and beyond the track was untouched, the snow unmarked. Pigs might fly?

Later, when the snow had melted and we returned for a visit, we noticed a wound in the trunk of the sycamore opposite the gate. The bark was scored and blackened as if from a burn. Ball lightning? A meteorite? I have searched the ground below the tree many times, and found nothing. I have a meteorite, a lump of what looks like iron, given to me long ago and kept with other treasures – bird-skulls, a goose's wing, fossils, shells and pebbles gathered from the ground and the shore – so I know what it might look like.

*

Flashback to October 1984 when I came to live here on my own to take up a one-year post as poet-in-residence at the university in Lampeter. It felt like my first big adventure since I had grown up and had children. Ten years of part-time teaching at Newport College of Art were over, David was working with an architectural practice in Aberystwyth, the 'children' had left our Cardiff home for university and onward. I was ready for a challenge. With Meg, my springer spaniel, for company, I moved in to our primitive ruin at the back of beyond, with no electricity or indoor plumbing, bottled gas for cooking and heating water, an iron stove for warmth. I felt excited, and very brave! Every day I thought of Marged: how had she survived here, cold and alone after the deaths of her Tadcu,[1] and her aunt. When I think of Marged's 'aunt' I am

---

1 grandfather.

more certain than ever that she was, in fact, her mother. In those old days, in a nineteenth-century chapel-going society, a pregnant, unmarried woman was never forgiven. Shame would have silenced the truth.

Every day I drove the twenty miles to Lampeter in my Renault 4 to work with students in the room assigned to me on College Road. That October was 'marigold', days in college busy with workshops and meeting poets and would-be poets among the students and from the town. Every morning before I left home I filled the coal bucket, replenished my water supply with buckets from the well, and filled the oil lamps. Back home to Blaen Cwrt every evening, I lit the stove and the lamps, locked myself and Meg safe inside the thick stone walls, and pretended to be Annie Dillard in *Pilgrim at Tinker Creek*, still among my favourite books, to read, re-read, and be inspired.

*

I often think of Annie Dillard, remembering how I met her once on a visit to the college where she taught in New England, and how together we climbed a hill marvellously named Lamentation Ridge. There, on the slope, we saw a garter snake. Annie picked it up and handed it to me. It felt cool, textured like raw silk, but alive, thrilling, a living, swirling S. It was like trying to hold a river still in my two hands as it twisted to be free. I set it down and we watched it flow free, away into the grass.

*

In October 2018, here at Blaen Cwrt, tree-planting plans are making progress. Some old trees – the sycamore and a dying ash tree by the drive, and, behind the house to the west, the too-close, over-reaching laburnums – have been felled. Now, after centuries in the dark, even in October the house basks in western evening light. It streams over our most recently acquired scrap of field, between the house-back and the lane, and, for the first time in over a hundred years, it shines into the sitting room through the big new window set in the back wall. The land, just a small field-corner, too narrow for Henbant's huge machines, they agreed to sell to us. With the bank and trees removed, our sitting room floods with late afternoon sunlight, and our terrace is no longer drowned in shadow every afternoon and evening. Now, even in October, late sun on the terrace, we enjoy a sip at the garden table after a day's work, and a fire in the Iron Man's belly to warm us. For the first time in more than a century of its existence, Blaen Cwrt, no longer backed into the hill, breathes easy in generous space. Even the rust-red, leaking old roof – which must soon be replaced – sits happily in the opened landscape.

October 2019

This October is not marigold. It is grey, with rain, floods, dark days. Will the dearest poetry lose all meaning as climate change destroys the seasons, and some of our most loved tree species die? Will all insects disappear? Will there never again be the need to remember and to say silently to myself lines from Keats's 'Ode to Autumn'?

> And still more, later flowers for the bees,
> until they think warm days will never cease.

The month opens with days of torrential showers, its rages interspersed with interludes of blazing sunlight, butterflies woken and on the wing, and now I am so dazzled here at the table that I must create a sunshade out of my opened umbrella and write in its shadow. And so it goes on, day after day, violent, violet rainstorms one after another sweeping in from the Atlantic, torn leftover rags of hurricanes from the Americas, broken by moments, sometimes hours, of blinding, low sun.

*

David is working on the root and bole of our late, lamented ash tree. I read somewhere that a tree-root can fill an area four to seven times larger than the tree crown occupies in the sky. Our great ash, our blackbird's old singing tree, was felled, sawn up, taken away over a year ago, emptying the sky of its cloudy crown of fronded boughs, and the drive and garden of its shade. But the huge rooted stump endures. It is a city. The tree showed every sign of death. Its leaves shrivelled, no foliage opened on its twigs and branches, the bark peeled from its trunk. Yet the roots hold fast. They seem sappy, as if they were still trying to send water from the deep earth to the crown. In its will to live it has put up two green stems. I had always thought of a tree trunk as a single pillar, yet hacking the ash root apart reveals it is composed of many rising trunks fused into one. It is strangely beautiful. The multiple pillars of its trunk rise, many-towered, an Italian hill town, a monastery built on a rock. The digging has revealed vast underground workings, the stuff that kept the tree alive and standing still grimly grasping the earth with all the stubborn power of its complex self. It refuses to let go and declare itself dead – I cannot think of it as a 'thing'. Months ago, a year since the tree's felling, David decided that the bole, still embedded at the end of the hedge-bank closest to our new small studio building, must be removed. For weeks he has spent hours every day with chainsaw, axe, spade, hand-saw, but there is still more than a giant's chair to be removed. What remains is taller than me, the bole monstrous, deep and wide, holding on with the old tree's hundred or more years of intelligent power, a huge tangle of roots grasping deep earth. The root ball has the volume of a grand piano. Trees nourish each other under the ground. They communicate.

*

This year, October rides the Atlantic on the diminishing power of a series of hurricanes born in the Americas, storms bearing black clouds of torrential rain to dump as soon as it reaches land. Rain hisses and clatters without cease on the roof and the terrace as the storm drags through. Then, silence, stillness, and now, as I write, sunlight spills gold over the garden. The maples are fire-red, the hazels gold, but the beech trees lost their leaves long before they had a chance to blaze with autumn colour, and there has been no autumn frost to fire the foliage, no 'marigold'. Instead, for colour we have hydrangeas, blues darkening to ink, and red fading to old rose, and their leaves all reddening too. A blazing sunset before their death. My favourite hydrangeas are the blue ones, a beautiful clear blue all summer, now deepening to purple. Two years ago I over-pruned the bushes, and too few flowers opened in summer to cut, bring in and stand in waterless vessels, their petals drying. Indoors the colour lasts all year, until there are new ones to cut and bring in to take their place. Our acidic, lime-free soil is the nourishment they need to keep them blue.

Every October I replace last year's flowers with fresh ones, as my mother always did when I was a child in our first house in Barry, and later, in Penarth. This year the bushes grew and flowered profusely, so I have a big yellow jug and two crocks full of October blue. I am tempted to bring in still more flower heads, now darkening from sky to ink-purple. Today it is David who remembers to gather them, heavy with rain, shaking drops from their heads as he crosses the lawn.

Blue Hydrangeas

You bring them in, a trug of thundercloud,
neglected in long grass and the sulk
of a wet summer. Now a weight of wet silk
in my arms like her blue dress, a load
of night-inks shaken from their hair –
her hair a flame, a shadow against light
as long ago she leaned to kiss goodnight
when downstairs was a bright elsewhere
like a lost bush of blue hydrangeas.
You found them, lovely, silky, dangerous,
their lapis lazulis, their indigoes
tide-marked and freckled with the rose
of death, beautiful in decline.
I touch my mother's skin. Touch mine.

25 October

Today marks one hundred and sixty years since the sinking of the Royal Charter, the fastest ship of its day. It sailed from Australia, in record time, carrying home the gold, the miners and their families. Almost at journey's end, and in sight of land, they were hit by a terrible storm, their ship driven onto the sands between Dulas Bay in Anglesey and Liverpool, to be wrecked in the shallows. Four hundred and fifty died. I should have been in Anglesey today for the commemoration, to read my poem, commissioned by an artist working with film and a choir, but I was in Tŷ Newydd, at the end of a good week tutoring poetry with Paul Farley, and a dynamic group of poets. It was great to tutor with Paul. He listens, lets them speak, encourages.

29 October

Home again, the month close to its end on a beautiful day. Warm and cloudless. The small acer at the end of the path – Euros's tree – is aflame. The big acer here in the garden is bare, its leaves scattered and shrivelled on the lawn. The beech trees hardly stir, stripped of all foliage since the false spring in February brought them to leaf too early, only to be killed by the unseasonal frost in May.

*

Despite October marigold, we are suffering political disaster, the dangerous political shift to the extreme right, the extreme left driving the deep divide, racism, division, ugly talk. We carry a cloud of sadness, and to endure it and recover we have to remind ourselves why. We dread the damage it will do, the increase in all the hardships loaded onto people by the Tories' years of 'Austerity'.

*

Hallowe'en. Boris's 'dead in a ditch' day if he didn't 'get Brexit done'. (He didn't.) I need a metaphor for survival, to defeat the overwhelming sadness, the ugly divisions we have never known before. I consider the ash tree-root. The root outgrows and outlives the dying tree. It is generous, unselfish. The Westminster politics tree is full of wind and clamour. It is no longer democratic, no longer just, no longer representative of the majority, no longer to be trusted. In its loud branches democracy is dead. The root is 'us', a system that nourishes its neighbours, a quiet underground movement. It is neighbourhood, community, the creative community, the worlds of the arts, family, friends. Everyone we know. Our friends in Europe. I share the idea with David. I learn that trees communicate underground, that their roots reach wide as the crown, and deep, deep down in the earth.

October 2020

> *'All changed, changed utterly:*
> *A terrible beauty is born'*
> 'Easter, 1916', W.B. Yeats

Summer is over. A clamour of crows flies east over the house, the garden, the land, hunting for flesh in fields where the last of the silage was gathered on late summer Bank Holiday Monday. Rooks, ravens, crows: corvids. It echoes the other word, the name of a new killer, the name of fear, the word on the air, down radio waves, in the morning *Guardian*. It is the black crow in our dreams every night and day since February, when it had already begun its predatory multiplication. Those who knew it months before did nothing to warn us, to stop its progress.

Autumn: confirmed cases and the death count rises, in Britain, and everywhere. In Wales, as I write, 25,000 cases are recorded, and deaths innumerable. Every death is a tragedy. To grieve for one person is simpler than to weep for thousands. The virus is a secret agent undermining our safety, our democracy. Anxiety grows as Covid on its covert way is echoed by talk of Russian and Chinese cyberattacks on our privacy, our security. One seems a metaphor for the other, both real and dangerous.

We have 'self-isolated' – a phrase for the times – for eight months here at Blaen Cwrt, among our beautiful eighteen acres of Ceredigion. Since early March I have seen only David, the postman, the picture restorer returning a painting, occasionally a neighbour from the farm across the valley, sometimes one of David's clients, Tomi and his men in the fields repairing fences. One golden October morning the sound of the chainsaw sings over the fields. When gates were opened, Gethin's sheep wandered the track into Cae Blaen Cwrt.

We are not alone or imprisoned, but free among our green acres in the company of a young fox, birds, rabbits, rodents, small, scuttling things, and a hare who lopes in, nibbles a grass stem and settles in its form on the other side of the lawn. Our adopted tortoiseshell cats, Mali and Medi, here for a month now, have settled so well they might have been born here. Not a rat or squirrel has been seen since their arrival, and the only mice are the corpses they bring us as gifts. They have done their job, clearing us of a plague of vermin which began with the death of our last cat, two years ago. Blaen Cwrt needs its cats. They come in from wandering to sleep in the sun.

When, in my lifetime, was there ever a silence like this? It is, indeed, 'a terrible beauty': silence, clean air, danger. With a creak the woodpecker arrives in a dazzle of scarlet, black and white; there's a click when the elegant little nuthatch comes: its profile of paired ellipses, from tips of curved beak to tail, contain all that a nuthatch is: heart, hunger, need, instinct, between its ink-blue back and rose-cream breast. It's gone in a flurry as a flight of corvids clears the garden. After months summering in the woods and fields, the birds are coming back to the garden.

*

The kettle comes to the boil for mid-morning tea. I make it, pour, carry it to the table where we work. For a while there is no sound but the ts, ts, of keys tapped, a breath, a pause for thought. The good silence of Us. We two and the cats are the whole world now. Trees fill the east and south glazed walls of the room where we work, glimpses of fields and distant hills show through tawny foliage of beech, acer, laburnum. The sky is perfect blue. Colour is autumnal: creeping wild geranium, the red acer, all but a hem of its foliage fallen, rose hydrangeas on the terrace, fading cream *Hydrangea paniculata*, and my favourite, the blue bush in the shady bed by the bank, under the reaching, dipping boughs of the great beech tree's flame-gold.

*

A circuit-breaker lockdown holds Wales together, safe, with one rule for us all, for two weeks, from Friday 23 until Saturday 7 November. Small birds have returned, looking for food. The shops have no peanuts, just seeds for the feeders, so I've sent for some online. All but food shops are closed, so birds must wait. The Covid cases are rising steeply, though not here, in Ceredigion.

I so look forward to the nuthatch returning to the tube we hang on the gutter outside the glass.

The Drowned Forest
November 2018

While trees are sleeping, I turn my mind to the haunted woodlands of mythology, history and archaeology, and, in particular, the ghostly upheaval of an ancient drowned forest on a beach in Ceredigion – a beach I know well. Cantre'r Gwaelod – the drowned hundred – was a land overwhelmed by the rising sea between four and a half and five thousand years ago. It is mythology and archaeology. It is story-telling and science.

For many years, the blackened remains of the forest have been visible at low tide on the long sandy beach at Borth, north of Aberystwyth. In the early 2000s, during a particularly violent Atlantic storm that raged straight in from the Irish Sea, and other storms in subsequent years, ever more frequent due to the increasing effects of global warming, huge tide-surges sucked and loosened tons of sand, washing it from the shore. These recent events have revealed, not just the scattered tree stumps that had long been visible, but much more: the blackened remains of what must have been a great forest, long since drowned by the sea and buried under sand. Between five and six and a half thousand years ago, the forest stretched from Borth to Ynyslas. Unearthed from below hardened peat, the remains of a wattle walkway supported by upright posts provide evidence that it must once have been a place of human habitation three or four thousand years ago. The remains show that people lived in the forest, and that they were forced to find ways to survive and to travel over ground which was becoming ever more waterlogged beneath their feet. History has become myth, and myth is history.

'Cantre'r Gwaelod' is a traditional Welsh story, passed down the centuries from adult to child across generations. Like all fairy tales the story was assumed to be 'just a myth'. Yet the story it tells is that long ago, somewhere along Cardigan Bay, a real community of forest-dwellers gradually lost their homeland to the sea. Recent events – rising seas, global warming, and fresh archaeological discoveries – demonstrate that the story arises from an unfolding disaster.

At the heart of magic and miracle, saint and symbol, in the archaeology of language, in place names, local stories and national mythologies, lies the truth, the evidence as solid as that provided by material objects excavated from the earth. All mythologies, including the Old and New Testaments of the Bible, have arisen from human accounts of real events as they were understood at the time of the first telling. The traditions of storytelling are a framework for words and images to convey what people experienced, believed and saw in their lifetime. Myth is fact as understood by an event's first witnesses, who pass the story on – and passing the story on is the art of storytelling, of recording a version of history. Myth's function is a way of human messaging. The narrative shifts from teller to listener, characters and events embellished in every generation with ever-changing detail of magic and colour, like all myths. But at the core of all the stories lies a truth. Something actually did happen, long ago. A witness found words to tell a listener, gave it life, coloured it with images. It was passed on, embellished with each telling, down the generations. Myth lives to tell the tale.

The legend of Cantre'r Gwaelod is the people's story. It tells of a country covered by forests which was gradually lost to the rising sea. Archaeology records that a forest of pine, alder, oak and birch had covered the land until it was submerged, probably in the sixth century B.C. Years ago, when I first saw the blackened branches of trees jutting from the sand on Borth beach near Aberystwyth, I began to wonder – was this the origin of Cantre'r Gwaelod, a story I had known since childhood? The myth long intrigued me, associated as it was with a beach which I knew. Looking along the beach I wondered about the legend and the black stumps of trees jutting from the sand at low tide. Was this the forest of legend? Archaeology has proved it was.

Some years ago, Gomer Press commissioned me to rewrite a version, in English, of a collection of stories by the Welsh children's writer, T. Lew Jones. His book is called *Lleuad yn Olau.* In my version, *One Moonlit Night,* along with the other tales in the collection, I retell the story of the drowned forest in my own words, following T. Llew Jones's account, at the same time keeping in mind the real drowned forest. Climate change, rising seas, and a particularly violent storm in February 2008, and another in 2014 which washed a vast tonnage of sand from the beach, have revealed further evidence. The remains of walkways were revealed, proving that 4,500 years ago a community of people had indeed lived and worked in the forest, constructing walkways to carry them over land growing more and more waterlogged. Mythology brings us the story. Archaeology proves it as fact.

When the *Guardian* proposed publishing poems about climate change, I knew that we must use our work and our words to make our views known. We must use poetry to protest.

Cantre'r Gwaelod

The morning after, the beach at Borth
is a graveyard, a blackened forest
thundered out of the sand by the storm,
drowned by the sea six thousand years ago
when the Earth was flat,
the horizon the edge of the world.

Relics of stilted walkways tell their story:
how they walked over water between trees
longing for a land lost when the sea-god stole it,
how they fled, shouldering children,
with every creature that could crawl, run, fly,
till time turned truth to myth.

It's how it will be as world turns reflective:
seas sated with meltwater, craving more;
a cliff-fall takes a bungalow; a monstrous
tide rips up a coastal train-track;
storm fells a thousand-year-old oak,
smashes a graceful seaside promenade.

Grieve for lost wilderness – for the lovesick salmon.
lured by sweet river water sleeved in the salt,
homing upstream to spawn at the source
where it was born; for mating hares
in love with the March wind; for thermals
lifting a flaunt of red kites over the wood;

for bees mooning for honey in weedless fields;
for drowsy marsh fritillary butterflies
swarming the ancient bog at Cors Llawr Cwrt;
for the brown hairstreak in love with blackthorn
and the honeydew of aphids in the ash;
for the blackbird's evening aria of possession;

for Earth's intricate engineering unpicked
like the flesh, sinews, bones of the mother duck
crushed on the motorway, her young
bewildered in a blizzard of feathers;
the balance of things undone by money,
the indifferent hunger of the sea.

November 2019

2 November

Noon at the table in Blaen Cwrt. A morning of torrential showers, flashes of gold light, wind in the trees. The acer at the end of the vista is a glory. It has been a morning of birds: a family of pigeons, flights of fieldfares, a visitation of long-tailed tits. We have filled the feeders for the regular visitors, wrens, robins, tits, finches, the spotted woodpecker, but the flocks are pausing, passing on. The pigeons peck on the grass. It is good to be home after two days in Cardiff. Hallowe'en, (Boris's 'dead-in-a-ditch' day) and my 'Poetry as Story Telling' session for the Open University, before a difficult drive home through dangerously lashing rain. The drive took four hours, instead of two. It is cold. I cook to get myself and the house warm: tortilla, cawl, Welsh cakes. We turn off the news – Blah-blah-blah!

9 November

It is dark at half past five. Too early for supper, or even a sip of something. Outside, to the east and south, is the black night and an after-rain silence. Torrents pass, spiteful and hissing. Yesterday – Friday – was a beautiful day. Tomorrow, gold is promised. All is change.

14 November

Wildfires in Australia. Floods in Venice, in Yorkshire, Derbyshire, the English flatlands. We are destroying our earth. 'Change and decay in all around I see.'

22 November

Brighton for Poetry Live tomorrow. The Holiday Inn – the sea on holiday crashing the burnt-black pier, licking the very windows of this room. Here for the first of Poetry Live's winter run, dinner with Imtiaz, Carol Ann, Tony, at an excellent seafood restaurant, after a long day. Cardiff to Southampton was good, but from Southampton to Brighton the train was poky and overcrowded, the journey long and slow. Yet all the way I met kind, helpful people.

27 November

Poetry Live in Bath, so easy from Cardiff. I arrived in time to pause for a coffee on my walk to the Forum. Home to Cardiff, to Roma, to David.

28 November

A journey through grey rain to Paddington, sinking deeper and deeper into the slough of despond at all that England offers in these dark times, to be cheered by a kind Asian taxi driver, tea and talk in the Barbican with Imtiaz, a sip of wine when Carol Ann returned from her long late farewell lunch with her gold-medal committee. Then supper at Carluccio's, and bed in the white room, sleeplessly watching the city, its glittering towers, stanchions and cranes, as wakeful as I was.

November 2020

4pm. Dark. Drear. November. It is my least favourite month. As our trees dissolve in darkness I conclude with trees, my tale of the drowned forest, my reimagining of a real, prehistoric event. It seems the best way to set it on the page.

The lights are on. The two cats haunt the table. David works opposite me. He has brought us mugs of tea. There is nothing left beyond this room. Darkness like a rising sea has taken the world away. A drowning forest. It is a creepy bedtime story.

*

The Country Under the Sea

Today Cardigan Bay is just part of the Irish Sea which flows into the great Atlantic Ocean, and waves lash the long curve of its shores from Aberdaron in the north to Fishguard in the south. To the north the Llŷn peninsula curves its arm about the bay, with Ynys Enlli[1] at its fingertip, raising a grey head from the waters. The old princedom of Dyfed embraces its southern shore.

Many centuries ago Cardigan Bay was not there. Where the grey seas break, there was once a green country of fertile fields, and there were dwellings, gardens, villages, cattle and sheep grazing, men and women at their work, and children playing. Today that fair country which we call Cantre'r Gwaelod lies drowned under the waters of Cardigan Bay.

Before it became a beautiful place to live, it had been a huge landlocked marsh that lay below sea level, always threatened by flood, until a strong wall was built to hold back the sea. At every high tide watchmen walked the wall to make sure the sea did not breach it. If, some stormy night, the sea should find its way between the stones, the watchmen would climb the tower that stood halfway along the wall, and they would ring the great bell. As soon as they heard the bell all the people would come to help mend the hole before the sea could flood their country.

From time to time, when the tide was high and a gale blew from the west, the sea did make a hole in the wall, but every time that happened the watchmen were alert and the people came quickly and closed the breach with heavy stones, so no harm came to their land.

Looking after the wall was such an important job that it was given to one of the country's most important men. The

1 Bardsey Island.

king of that land, Gwyddno Garanhir, appointed his son, Prince Seithenyn, as Keeper of the Wall.

Years went by and the seas washed harmlessly against the wall. People worked the land and lived happily in Cantre'r Gwaelod. One wild autumn night a banquet was held in the Hall of King Gwyddno. It was his daughter's birthday and the king invited the gentry of Cantre'r Gwaelod to the feast. Festivities began early in the afternoon and went on late into the night, and by nightfall Prince Seithenyn had taken too much wine. The prince was drunk.

That night the highest tide of the year was expected, and the wind rose quickly and blew strongly from the west. The two young watchmen were walking the wall and looking out to sea. They had waited many hours to be relieved by another shift of watchmen, but no one came. The rest, like their prince, were at the feast, and were drunk.

The wind increased to a storm-force gale and the tide rose higher. There ought to have been more watchmen than usual on the wall that night as the hurricane and the high tide together were more than usually dangerous. The two young men walked to the tower halfway along the wall where the great bell would toll if the sea breached the defences. There was no need to ring it yet, but high tide was still to come, so they decided that one of them should go to fetch more men to help with the watch. The watchmen's horses were stabled under the tower, and soon one man was galloping through the dusk towards the Hall of King Gwyddno.

The other young guard, a boy called Gwyn ap Llywarch, waited nervously in the tower as night fell fast. The sea was seething up against the wall and white foam filled the air. The boy could hear the waves drumming on the wall and his heart thudded with fear. He thought of the banquet at the hall, and the king's beautiful daughter, dancing at the feast in her finest clothes. Although he was the only son of a gentleman without fortune, he was in love with Mererid, the king's daughter.

That moment, he longed to be in the hall dancing with her.

High tide came. The sea raged and lightning flashed through the darkness, illuminating the waves. Gwyn's companion was a long time coming back, so he ran from the tower and into the stables to make sure his horse was calm.

When he returned to the wall, he saw, in a flash of lightning, a sight to set his hair on end. The sea had breached the wall, and white water flowed in a wild torrent between the stones. He could hear the rattle of boulders as they shifted under the force of the waves, and the sound of rushing water. The wall had broken. He ran down the steps and into the tower and hauled the rope of the great bell. It tolled and tolled across the land and the sea and was swallowed by the storm.

But that night no one was listening, no one came to save the wall. Gwyn ap Llywarch ran down to the stables, leapt onto the back of his horse, and galloped towards the hall. He reached the gates of the king's house in safety, and at once heard a tumult of singing and laughter. Inside he saw an astonishing sight. The king, the noblemen and all the soldiers were drunk, many so inebriated that they lay snoring and insensible, and Seithenyn, Keeper of the Wall, more drunk than anyone.

Gwyn shouted with all his strength, 'The sea has breached the wall!'

Some of the revellers looked at him, amazed, while others laughed. Where was Princess Mererid? Gwyn went to the room where the women were, and he saw her, flushed with pleasure and dressed in velvet and lace.

'Come with me quickly!' he said to her. 'The sea has breached the wall and is drowning the land. We must get to the hills.'

The smile died on the Princess's face. She looked at Gwyn in confusion. He took her hand and they ran together through the banqueting hall towards the door of the court, and as they went he shouted at the top of his voice: 'Make for the hills! The sea is flooding the land! The wall has broken!'

He ran from the hall to the porch where the horse was tethered, and soon he and Mererid were galloping through rain and wind and darkness.

By now at least some of the revellers understood what had happened, and were trying to flee from the sea which rolled over the fields and plains of their beautiful country.

As dawn broke, Gwyn ap Llywarch and Princess Mererid were safe on a high crag over Aberarth in Ceredigion, gazing westwards over the water. Beside them grazed the tired horse which had carried them safely to the hills. They looked down on a tragic sight. There was no sign now of the great sea wall, nor of the tall tower that had stood at its centre; no sign of the hall of the king, nor of the villages, the forest, the green fields.

There was nothing left but the grey and rolling waves of the sea. They gazed for a long time, tears pouring down their cheeks, until at last Gwyn said: 'Princess, everyone, everything I love has gone. The cruel sea has taken it all. But at least we have each other. We must stay together and build a new home and a new life in these hills.'

'We will, Gwyn', she replied, and she took his hand and they turned their backs on Cantre'r Gwaelod forever.

Hibernation
December 2018

Leaf-fall. Darkness. The weather colder, days darker. Daylight shrinks minutes every day, the closer we get to the winter solstice. All deciduous trees are sleeping, the great root system that keeps a tree fed and watered shut down in hibernation. If we slept for half of every year, would we live as long as trees? I examine a beech branch for its sleeping leaf buds. They dream the future, as they have done every year of the tree's long life, and, before it, this tree's ancestor whose seeds fell to earth centuries ago, to germinate, and make our beech. I share but a moment of its life on earth.

*

On winter evenings, supper over, we clear the table, turn out the lights, leaving the glass-and-oak room to the night garden, to a passing fox, a hare, the sleeping trees, sometimes with the moon in their branches. Through the door in the thick stone wall between our 'new' kitchen-living-dining room and down two steps into our sitting room we step into history, from our bright new space into the old longhouse, into what was once the 'kitchen', where, a hundred years ago and more, the family lived, cooked, ate, and where Marged's grandfather slept in a cupboard bed.

Beside the sofa is a small oak cupboard, a surface for a reading lamp, a book, somewhere to set a glass down. It is the first lamp to be switched on in the evening as we step into the old house, which has settled itself more deeply into the earth than the architecture of our bright, light new spaces. Lamps lit, curtains drawn, flames leap in the wood burner.

These winter nights we have a regular visitor. A queen wasp. Nightly, she emerges from her hibernation somewhere behind our sofa, where she has sheltered since, at summer's end, her entire retinue died. Like a tree, her body contains the future. The seeds of the coming summer, her household, her swarm, her hive, with its magnificent wax city of honey cells, are stored in her tiny body. Woken by the warmth and light of the lamp, she emerges for a spell of preening. She is calm, preoccupied, almost tame, without any need to attack or fly away. After watching her night after night I have become fond of her, and protective. I must ensure her safety. Our future depends on her. I record her actions and her story. Back in the spring, or early summer, we noticed a wasp scraping tiny filaments from the lapped timber cladding at the gable end of the extension to our house.

Queen

She walks, stirred from the hushed dust
of a curtain-fold, steps out to preen,
summer's future in her winter dream.
We're careful not to crush or brush aside
the pregnant queen. She clings to my finger
as I set her safe beside my open book,

settles herself in yellow lamplight
to clean her six hinged limbs,
abdomen, mandibles, helmet of black and gold,
multiple eyes, thorax, wings of spun glass
veined like petals of wild plum, quince,
apple trees fertilised on humming days.

Her wintering body is a citadel
of a thousand cells. In spring she'll build
her palace from spittle and cellulose
scraped from the timbers of our house,

and lay her eggs in a thousand cradles,
pulsing with the humdrum drums of summer.

*

Remembering! When I was a child, close to Christmas, my father arrived from his travels round Wales as a BBC sound engineer bringing a tree. On Christmas Eve he brought it in, set in a tub of garden soil, and together we decorated it with home-made angels and a crib. In my early childhood we attached real candles to its branches, in holders with metal clips. Placed beneath the tree were gifts wrapped in smoothed-out Christmas paper saved from last year. I remember an antique doll with hinged limbs and a hollow china head, eyes that opened and shut as I lifted or laid her down. Where is she now? My Ga gave me a tiny green and white china teaset on its own little tray. I have it still. Shops were short of stuff, and old things were all that could be found. Beautiful things. That Christmas, or maybe that other snowy winter, 1947, I had an antique wooden music box which my father bought in a house sale or a junk shop. It was beautiful, with a leaf-pattern inlaid in its lid. To wind it up I had to raise the brass lever seven times – no more or I might break the spring – and it played six French tunes, its revolving brass barrel plucking the keys as it turned. Still, and silent now, it stands on the top of a carved chest in our bedroom. I dust it. I promise myself that at Christmas I will lift it down, and play those six French melodies, their titles now illegible, in faded brown ink on a page inside the lid. But when I hear them, I will know their names.

My sister was born on 2 January 1942. My mother went away to the hospital, and I was looked after rather erratically by my three childless aunts, my father's older sisters, Ceri, Phyllis and Doris, and by Ga, my grandmother, who came to stay for a while. War and rumours of war murmured over the snow from every radio in the house. There were men called air-raid wardens in the streets, on the lookout for enemies: I called the Nazis 'Nasties'. Sometimes we heard the long wailing cry of an air-raid warning. Sometimes I was put to bed with an eiderdown and a Teddy bear in the cupboard under the stairs, to be safe from the bombs. A few days after my mother came home with the baby, my father took me and Ga to Pembrokeshire to stay on the farm, safely far from Barry and its docks. On a flying day-visit to 'look after' me Doris brought me a doll with eyes that opened and closed. I named her Shirley, after the child film star, Shirley Temple.

I was sent to school in Barry when I was four, and it was there, in the hall of St Baruc's School, that I first saw our world, with its continents and oceans. It spun at the touch of a finger. I begged my father to get me one, and that year I had a globe for Christmas. He was pleased that I wanted such a thing. He was a traveller. He had been a 'Sparks', a wireless officer on merchant navy ships before he joined the BBC as a sound engineer, so he was pleased to teach me the names of countries he had visited and oceans he had sailed. When I spun the globe it showed me the seas and land that shaped the world, turning, my father told me, as our real earth did in its place in the universe – a word to keep me sleepless for hours. We lived in Flatholm, Lakeside, Cold Knap, Barry, Glamorgan, Wales, ending with 'The Universe'. It was written on the first page of all my favourite books. Did our parents teach us to recite our address, in case we got lost? Or did we love to record and be certain of every detail of our place on the turning surface of the world? The world was the globe in my bedroom, and there, among the continents and the oceans, between the North and South Poles, in its place between the warp and weft of latitudes and longitudes, was Flatholm, our house, too small to see. But it was there, and I was inside it.

All the science I knew came from my father. He explained the universe to me. He told me that all sound caught by his microphones was carried on forces called 'long waves', and how that sound was borne up on the waves to touch the lowest layer of the ionosphere, to be deflected back to earth and into our wireless sets. We had one in every room of our house. The lowest layer of the ionosphere – I loved the word 'ionosphere', and I still do – was called the Heaviside layer. The term made me imagine a carthen in the sky, a traditionally patterned and woven Welsh wool blanket that topped my bed - there was a carthen on everyone's bed – and it weighed so heavily I could hardly move my toes. I still see the ionosphere as a carthen in space. When I am dead, will I be able to move my toes?

Many years later I learned, to my great delight, that the Heaviside layer was not named for its weight, but for the scientist who discovered it, a Professor Heaviside, and that it has no connection, even metaphorically, with the carthen I had imagined wrapped around the earth to keep it warm. What serendipity to be so named and to follow such a science!

1 December 2019

Poetry Live. Three gigs done: Brighton Dome, Bath Forum and London Apollo Victoria Theatre. Manchester and Leeds to go. The prospect of travelling the long slow way to Manchester across the winter landscape fills me with profound homesickness and a sense of displacement, although I know the gloom will be alleviated by my arrival in the bright foyer of a hotel, and the prospect of dinner with my dear friend, Imtiaz Dharker.

In these dire times, every news report, every word spoken by those who would be king, casts me deeper into anxiety. The slough of despond. Lonely places seen from the passing train, places I don't know, houses where strangers live, nameless and foreign to me, have always darkened my spirits and filled me with unspecified longing. I tap this at the table in our bright, warm, little living room in our flat in Cardiff, and David's hands move silently as he works on his computer opposite me. It is a beautiful day. The stirred waters of the Ely below are blue with reflected sky. The sun is on the Garth and the foothills of the Beacons further distant. I have walked those hills. The bare trees on the Penarth side of the river are sunlit, unmoving in their winter sleep. I know them too. I am home.

*

Yesterday we drove the short distance over the river to Penarth, to visit the good independent bookshop, and the wonderful greengrocer next door which we discovered last week. It has the best display of fruit and vegetables I have seen for a very long time. I have packed two boxes with figs, baby aubergines, peppers, and strangely beautiful mushrooms like clusters of living pearls, as far-too-early Christmas presents for Imtiaz and Carol Ann. The two boxes fill my little suitcase, with my few clothes pushed into the gaps around them. Writing such things has burned dark energy, cheering me a little. I close this journal to get a little lunch for me and David, before he takes me, my luggage and my heavy heart to the station for my train to Manchester.

3 December

After endless rain the weather is fresher, colder, lovelier. The train to Manchester on Sunday was so overcrowded that there were people standing in the aisle the whole way. As always, a lonely gloom descended. What does it mean? Where does it come from? First I am nervous, rechecking times, tickets, platforms, luggage. Then homesickness rolls in like mist over the land, a heavy darkness in my soul, despite a beautiful sunset that lasted until its very last rose moment over the alien landscapes through which the train passed. The fields belong to strangers. The cities look lonely. I don't know the names of the streets. No one I know lives in those houses.

Yesterday, in the green room of the Olympia Theatre, Manchester, waiting to go on stage I had a conversation with Carol Ann about the homesickness I experience on winter train journeys, the bleakness at the sight of strange towns, unfamiliar landscapes. She was curious, helpful, saw a subject for poems in it. I wrote in my notebook: 'Journeys'. A start! Perhaps a sequence of poems. I have no idea where such a poem-journey might take me. At the moment the train seems to be heading towards the crash of next Thursday's elections. Maybe half of Britain feels this dread. Sometimes I think it is the journey called Life, heading to a strange country, maybe Death, that bleak place to which we will all be exiled.

Back to Cardiff, and a lovely day with David, happy again, the two of us working respectively at writing and architecture as the sun shone on the river, the Garth mountain, the white farms. Once, commissioned to write a poem for a painting by Evan Walters, I wrote about an old memory that often comes to me as I see a farmhouse across landscapes known and unknown, even in the familiar view from this table over the river Ely, the city, suburbs and the fields to the Garth mountain. A white farm stirs something remembered, forgotten, haunting, and it haunts me now.

Landscape with Farm

There is always a white farm
somewhere between you and the horizon,
a hundred fields folded under a sky
of scudding cloud. A hamlet, a church tower,
broken-backed barn and fallen walls dissolve
and light converges in one glowing gable,
the bright brow that holds all the light in the world.

You pause a moment, imagining life
in the white farm, bread rising in a crock
by the fire, a kettle coming into song,
an oilcloth on the table laid for tea
with china cups and saucers, the door open
for sunlight to step in, or a red hen.
Voices in the yard.

You're half-remembering, a cool kitchen,
a rug of sunlight on a flagstone floor.
A woman comes and goes. Your heart's in this,
but move on before the mountain takes the sun,
the white farm is returned to darkness,
and the only light left anywhere
is the first star.

7 December

Home to Blaen Cwrt. The house has survived our twelve-day absence. We turn into the drive with relief to see it is still here, and inside not a thing has been touched, a vase of flowers only just beginning to fade, a scatter of petals on the table.

*

For a few days I have carried some good news about elm trees, read on my travels: there is fresh hope for the tree, and sapling elms, resistant to the insect-borne disease that killed elm trees across Britain, are at this moment being bred, and one has been planted somewhere in Britain. There is hope that the elm can be brought back to our landscape. Plans are afoot for saplings to be sent to schools for children to plant. No one alive will see them reach their full height, but I don't care. I can dream them, imagine them, remember them, look at their images in paintings. I don't want to walk out of a dying earth. I want to be here to watch our young woodland flourish; I want to plant three elm trees on the Fron, to see their first spring, to share with Browning his 'Home-Thoughts from Abroad', where he notes that in April, '... the lowest boughs and the brushwood sheaf, Round the elm-tree bole are in tiny leaf'.

*

The past weeks' darkness has lifted from my soul like dissolving mist, and I see trees, trees, trees in clearing sunlight. A magpie spent many minutes in its old nest this morning, moving, turning, maybe tidying up? A flock of starlings settled in our remaining ash tree as we had breakfast, lifted and whirred away. And two blackbirds – male and female – crossed the terrace, one after another. A pair.

13 December

Friday 13, 2019. Electoral catastrophe. Darkness is back. Or is it a forest fire this time? Rage is healthier than gloom, and every friend and every stranger I admire shares this rage. Every email I receive, from poetry acquaintances in Ireland, Italy, London, from close family and good friends, a shared hurt at what Westminster has already done and the destruction they will wreak, the sickness, the need and the sorrow they will ignore. Rough sleepers. Homelessness. Child poverty. A burnt earth. All 'collateral damage'. They woo the voters in the north of England with their lies, and ignore Wales.

14 December

At three o'clock in the afternoon the sky is one expanse of grey, without cloud-edge, without movement. Stillness, then a sudden stir ruffles the winter hydrangeas, the leafless trees. Last night we were cold, and I lay wakeful. I slept at last, woke, slept again. I wonder how many millions of people in Britain are disturbed, not functioning, not sleeping, feeling sad and anxious today? After a politics-free day, until the 10 o'clock news, that is, comes the reckoning, and it is dark indeed.

Consolation: wisdom and humour in the *Guardian*, Dead Ringers on Radio 4, and the concept of 'Us' which I am nurturing in the metaphor of the tree-root. I need to think of the millions of people who feel as we do, and to be consoled by it. I am trying to clear my heart and mind of dark things, to concentrate on 'Us'.

*

Last night I saw and heard David talking to something or someone in this room. 'Ah! There you are!' he said. I came to look. He was speaking to a wren perched on the back of the sofa, before opening the glass doors to shoo it out. It must be Christmas, if the wren is here, searching for a tree to perch on indoors, ten days too soon. The tree lies on the terrace, awaiting its hour.

At four o'clock, dusk darkening the land, after we spent all day listening to Christmas music from all over the world on Radio 3 and suddenly we notice snow falling on the rooflights, obscuring the glass. Beautiful. According to the weather map we are on the western edge of a snowfall covering Britain.

*

Dark times. Australia burns. Indonesia drowns. 'Boristics' hurts. It is ugly. We must act together as a great 'Us', an underground community. As trees do.

Christmas Day

Just 'Us'. The sun shone. All was still. We listened to music, feasted, sipped, enjoyed the tiny painting by Roger Cecil we bought each other, our third painting by this artist. The first, the first work of art I had ever bought, it was fifty years ago from The Albany Gallery in Cardiff. I spent savings and the housekeeping money on it, so it must have cost under twenty quid, a snowy Valleys town with figures, in his characteristic early black, grey, white and mustard-gold, a streetscape under a tawny moon – or is it a dull gold mountain above the pit shaft and the street?

27 December

Owain came to stay, bringing Ifan with him. We all had supper together, then Ifan's girlfriend, Ella, called to collect him for a weekend with friends in somebody's holiday house in Aberporth. Ella is spectacular! She is nineteen, tall, splendid, and black, a warm London girl, and a talented singer. Owain stayed two nights with us, and helped David with work on the studio building.

31 December

New Year's Eve. Owain and Claire have been to hear Ella's choir sing evensong in Westminster Abbey, and they report that it was beautiful. Here, tonight, darkness but for tree-lights, the lights on the table and along the shelf over the glass walls, reflected again and again in the glass against the black night. Supper is cooking. Dylan is here, and he, David and I are together at the start of the 2020s, to sip, talk, listen, to see the old year out and the new year in.

7 January 2020

Written on a wild, wet morning, one day after Twelfth Night, as the decade turns. Our Christmas tree lies in the rain on the terrace, as sad a sight as the fallen anywhere. The lights, the baubles, the angels and the glitter are packed into two old wine boxes marked 'Christmas', to be stowed in the loft for next year. Our world is wounded. Australia is burning. Indonesia is flooded. The polar glaciers are melting. Oceans are choked with plastic.

Here in Ceredigion, 'the rain it raineth every day'. I write on a dark day at my usual place at the table. To the east, all land past the border of our closest field, Cae Blaen Cwrt, drowns in drizzle. South, beyond the terrace, two beech trees against a grey sky mark our small world's end, Llanllwni mountain and the miles of country between obliterated.

As we un-decked the hall, at the end of a stormy year for the world, for politics, for Britain, in the United States, in Europe, in the Middle East, and most of all on Planet Earth, like so many others I felt a helpless sorrow at the state of things. I urgently needed to lift from my heart the weight of broken Britain, of international disaster and bad governments. The world is burning, drowning, starving, yet the rich are sated with money. We need change, and a philosophy to get us through.

*

The day after Epiphany, trees have brought me what my mind yearns. For the past two years, far from the cacophony of politics, we have been preoccupied with our new woodland: 4,300 saplings. They help us dream: spring and a first leaf. Just when I most need a new way to imagine Britain in its current condition, especially the little country where we live, the young woodland and our old, dead ash tree offer me a metaphor.

The ash is felled; the root endures half-buried in the bank. It takes as much space underground in the dark as the crown did in the air. The bole is not a single stem grown to giant proportions, the one great bole with all its age-rings on view as I had imagined. It is a many-towered medieval hill town anchored to its root, self-governing, communal, neighbourly. It nourishes itself and others. Many parts have conjoined to form the trunk. I bring in a 'foot', a 'claw'. It is a piece of the ash tree where growth, maybe several stems welded as one, maybe the severed ends of roots, maybe a sawn-off giant's limb, an amputation, has become found art. Sculpture. A beautiful fragment that lies palm up, its claws spread open on the oak chest, cupping sunlight.

The root of the felled ash tree is a neighbourhood, a community. Us. It shows how small countries can continue, far from bad and failing government. The dying tree was felled four years ago. The root has outlived it to pass nourishment to its neighbours. It goes on 'while dynasties pass'.

2020

Winter Solstice, 21 December

The Year's Midnight

The flown, the fallen,
the golden ones,
the deciduous dead, all gone
to ground, to dust, to sand,
borne on the shoulders of the wind.

Listen! They are whispering
now while the world talks,
and the ice melts,
and the seas rise.
Look at the trees!

Every leaf-scar is a bud
expecting a future.
The earth speaks in parables.
The burning bush. The rainbow.
Promises. Promises.

ACKNOWLEDGEMENTS

'Why I Write': Radio 3, *The Verb*. Hay Festival, 2015.
'Tramp: Nothing is unless it has a word': Unpublished
'Slate': Radio 3, *The Verb*. Published in *Cornerstones: Subterranean Writings*, 2014.
'Something Understood': Lecture, Bristol conference: 'Man, Mystery, Myth and Metaphor, Poetry and the Heavens'. A version of this essay was published in *Heavenly Discourses*, edited by Nicholas Campion, 2016.
'Dylan Thomas: Music and Truth': adapted from talks and articles for Dylan Thomas's centenary, 2014.
'Return to Cold Knap Lake': published in *The Use of English*, 2016.